The
New England
Cookbook

The
New England
Cookbook

Jane Putnam Littlefield

GALLERY BOOKS
An imprint of W.H. Smith Publishers Inc.
112 Madison Avenue
New York, New York 10016

ISBN: 0–8317–6341–8

Published in the United States by
Gallery Books
An Imprint of W.H. Smith Publishers, Inc.
112 Madison Avenue
New York, New York 10016

This book was designed and produced by
Footnote Productions Ltd.
6 Blundell Street
London N7 9BH

Color origination by Hong Kong Scanner Craft, Ltd.
Printed by Lee Fung Asco Printers, Ltd.

✻ Contents ✻

❧ Appetizers ❧

Often called by the English name "starters" by the more traditional New Englanders, these small, delectable first courses prepare the appetite for the meal that lies ahead. In New England, seafood is often served as an appetizer—especially such deliciously convenient seafood as shellfish and shrimp. Favorite New England recipes for Stuffed Clams, Shrimp Cups and Deep-Fried Codfish Balls are given here, along with more unusual New England specialties such as Pickled Mussels. No matter what the recipe, the fresher the seafood is, the better it will taste.

An appetizer should stimulate the appetite, not sate it. Serve comfortable, not overwhelming, portions. However, almost any recipe in this chapter can easily be increased to accommodate unexpected guests or unexpected appetites. And when served with a salad and a loaf of crusty bread, many appetizers, such as Deviled Clams, can be a meal in themselves. For family meals and small gatherings, just one appetizer should be tantalizing enough. For larger groups, serve two or more complementary appetizers.

❧ Cheese Puffs

1 cup sifted flour
1 teaspoon baking powder
½ teaspoon salt
½ teaspoon dry mustard
2 eggs, separated
½ cup milk
1 cup grated Cheddar cheese
1½ cups vegetable oil

Sift the flour, baking powder, salt and dry mustard together into a bowl and set aside.

Beat the egg yolks in a small bowl and add the milk. Stir this mixture into the dry ingredients and combine thoroughly. Add the grated cheese to the mixture.

Beat the egg whites in a separate bowl and fold them into the batter.

Heat the oil in a skillet until it is very hot (365°–370°). Drop the batter by teaspoons into the oil and fry until golden brown. Remove and drain on paper towels.

Use Vermont Cheddar cheese to give your puffs a mellow, tangy flavor.

serves 6

❧ Deep-Fried Codfish Balls

1 pound salt codfish
2 cups mashed potatoes
¾ teaspoon freshly ground black pepper
½ teaspoon grated nutmeg
4 eggs, beaten
1½ cups vegetable oil

Soak the codfish in cold water for 4 hours, changing the water after 2 hours.

Drain the fish, place it in a pot, cover with fresh water and bring to the boil. Drain and flake the fish. Combine it with the mashed potatoes, pepper, and nutmeg. Add the eggs and mix thoroughly.

Heat the oil in a heavy skillet until it is very hot (375°). Drop the fish mixture by teaspoons into the oil and fry until golden brown.

The English explorer Bartholomew Gosnold gave Cape Cod its name in 1602 for the great abundance of codfish in the waters there. In 1640, Pilgrim colonists exported more than 300,000 dried codfish.

serves 6 to 8

✂ Pickled Mussels

3 quarts mussels
2 or 3 onions, thinly sliced
3 or 4 cloves garlic, crushed
mixed pickling spices
salt to taste
freshly ground black pepper to taste
cider vinegar or white wine vinegar

Wash, scrub, and debeard the mussels thoroughly. Steam them open in a large pot with 1 cup water.

Lift out the mussels and shells, reserving the broth.

In a large crock or glass jar arrange layers of shelled mussels, onion slices, garlic, pickling spices, salt, and pepper. Fill the container with strained mussel broth to one-third its depth, then add vinegar to cover.

Let the container stand, uncovered, for at least 3 days before serving. Stir once or twice.

serves 10 to 12

✂ Deviled Clams

½ cup diced onion
½ cup diced celery
½ cup finely chopped green pepper
4 tablespoons butter
2 tablespoons flour
1 tablespoon freshly grated Romano cheese
⅛ teaspoon salt
⅛ teaspoon white pepper
½ teaspoon Worcestershire sauce
1 dash Tabasco sauce
2 dozen plain crackers, crushed
1 6-ounce can minced clams

Melt the butter in a skillet. Add the onion, celery and green pepper and sauté until the onion is transparent but not browned.

Stir in the flour, cheese, salt, white pepper, Worcestershire sauce and Tabasco sauce, stirring vigorously to blend to an even consistency. Add ½ cup of the cracker crumbs and mix. Add the minced clams with their juice, and cook slowly until the mixture thickens.

Preheat the oven to 350°.

Spoon the mixture into clam shells (real or ceramic) or small ovenproof bowls.

Melt another tablespoon of butter in the skillet and stir in the remaining bread crumbs. Sprinkle the crumbs over the filled shells or bowls. Bake until lightly browned, about 15 minutes.

serves 4

✂ Stuffed Clams

24 medium cherrystone or little neck clams
4 large mushrooms, chopped
4 tablespoons butter
salt to taste
freshly ground black pepper to taste
½ cup freshly grated Parmesan cheese
3 parsley sprigs
2 lemons, halved

Open the clams and shell them. Wash the meat and shells thoroughly. Remove the meat and set the shells aside.

Preheat the oven to 350°

Chop the clams and mix them with the mushrooms, 3 tablespoons of butter, salt and pepper. Stuff the clam shells with the clam mixture. Sprinkle them with the cheese and dot with the remaining butter.

Place the filled shells in a baking pan and bake until golden brown on top, about 15 minutes. Serve garnished with parsley sprigs and lemon halves.

serves 4 to 6

❧ Baked Oysters

24 large oysters
2 tablespoons butter
salt to taste
freshly ground black pepper to taste
2 teaspoons chopped chives

Preheat the oven to 375°.

Scrub the oysters well. Place, them, unopened, in a deep baking pan and bake for 2 to 3 minutes until they open.

Remove the upper half of the shell. Place a bit of butter, salt, pepper and some chopped chives on each oyster and return the pan to the oven for 3 minutes more. Serve piping hot.

serves 4 to 6

❧ Baked Oysters with Bacon

24 oysters
6 to 8 bacon slices
freshly ground black pepper to taste
butter

Fry the bacon slices until they are very lightly browned but not crisp. Drain on paper towels.

Preheat the oven to 375°.

Open the oysters. Leave the meat in the bottom shells and reserve the top shells. Place the oysters in a shallow baking pan, using the top shells to steady them. Make sure the oysters are level and steady. Dust the oysters with pepper and dot with butter.

Cut the bacon slices into quarters. Top each oyster with a bacon piece.

Bake until the oysters curl at the edges, about 5 to 8 minutes. Serve garnished with lemon wedges and parsley sprigs.

serves 4 to 6

❧ Scallop Brochettes

2 tablespoons finely grated onion
2 tablespoons lemon juice
salt to taste
freshly ground black pepper to taste
1 pound sea scallops
4 small onions, halved
8 bacon slices, cut in half
8 white mushroom caps
3 tablespoons melted butter

Put the grated onion, lemon juice and a dusting of salt and pepper in a bowl. Add the scallops, toss and let marinate for 40 minutes at room temperature.

Drain the scallops, reserving the marinade. Thread the scallops alternately with the mushrooms, bacon and onion onto 8 metal skewers.

Preheat the broiler to high.

Broil the brochettes, basting them with the melted butter and reserved marinade until the bacon is crisp and the scallops white and firm, about 10 minutes. Turn the brochettes often to cook on all sides. Serve garnished with slices of lemon.

serves 4

✂ Cold Shrimp Cups

2 cups mayonnaise
2 teaspoons grated onion
2 garlic cloves, crushed
1 ripe tomato, peeled, seeded and chopped
2 tablespoons brandy
8 large shrimp, cooked, shelled, deveined and
  very coarsely chopped

Put the mayonnaise, onion, garlic, tomatoes and brandy into a mixing bowl and mix together. Add the shrimp. Toss vigorously and chill.

Serve in crystal goblets or bowls lined with lettuce leaves.

serves 6

✂ Puffed Shrimp

12 large shrimp, cooked, shelled and deveined
1 egg white
¼ cup freshly grated Parmesan cheese
salt to taste
cayenne pepper to taste
⅛ teaspoon paprika
½ cup mayonnaise
12 slices whole wheat bread

Cut the shrimp in half lengthwise.

Beat the egg white in a mixing bowl until it is stiff but not dry. Fold in the cheese, salt, cayenne pepper, paprika and mayonnaise.

Lightly toast the bread. Cut each slice in half diagonally. Spread each half with the egg white mixture. Top each with a halved shrimp. Arrange the bread halves on a large baking sheet.

Preheat the broiler to high.

Broil until the topping is puffed and a light, golden-brown color, about 2 to 3 minutes.

serves 6

✂ Apple Slices and Bacon

1 pound sliced bacon
6 large tart apples, cored and sliced
½ cup flour
½ cup sugar
1 teaspoon grated nutmeg

In a large skillet fry the bacon until crisp. Remove the bacon and drain on paper towels. Drain all but ¼ cup of the bacon fat from the skillet.

Combine the flour, sugar and nutmeg in a bowl. Dredge the apple slices in the flour mixture and fry them in the bacon fat until golden brown, turning frequently. The apples are done when they are easily pierced with a fork. Serve with the bacon slices.

serves 6

✂ Cheese Straws

1 cup grated Parmesan cheese
1 cup flour
1 tablespoon melted butter
1 egg yolk, beaten
salt to taste
cayenne pepper to taste

Preheat the oven to 450°.

Combine the flour and cheese in a mixing bowl. Add the salt and cayenne. Add the beaten egg yolk and the melted butter. Mix gently to form a paste.

Roll the dough out onto a lightly floured surface to ⅛-inch thickness. With a pastry wheel or sharp knife, cut the dough into strips 4 inches long. Place the strips on heavily greased baking sheets and bake unti light brown, about 5 to 7 minutes. Cool slightly and remove from the sheets.

serves 6 to 8

✁ Cheese Spread

1 cup cottage cheese
½ cup milk
½ cup cream
1 teaspoon salt
½ teaspoon black pepper
¼ cup chopped watercress

Put the cottage cheese in a bowl. Slowly pour in the milk and cream, mixing with the back of a spoon. Blend to the consistency of a medium-soft paste while adding the salt, pepper and watercress. Serve with bread.

serves 4 to 6

✁ Shrimp Fritters

1 pound uncooked shrimp, shelled and coarsely
   chopped
1 cup flour
1 teaspoon baking powder
½ teaspoon salt
¼ teaspoon black pepper
2 eggs, beaten
½ cup milk
⅓ cup finely chopped onion
½ teaspoon Tabasco sauce
oil for deep frying

In a mixing bowl combine the flour, baking powder, salt and pepper. Stir in the eggs and sufficient milk to make a thick batter. Add the onion, Tabasco sauce and shrimp. Mix until the shrimp pieces are well coated.

Heat the oil to 375° in a deep skillet. Drop the batter by teaspoons into the oil. Fry until golden brown, about 2 minutes.

Serve hot with cocktail sauce or tartar sauce.

serves 6

✁ Crab Cakes

3 tablespoons butter
¾ cup finely chopped onion
1 cup soft breadcrumbs
1 pound crabmeat, flaked and cleaned
3 eggs, beaten
¾ teaspoon salt
1 teaspoon dry mustard
1 teaspoon Worcestershire sauce
1 to 2 tablespoons light cream
½ cup flour
olive oil for frying
lemon wedges

In a large skillet melt the butter and add the onions. Cook until the onions are soft but not brown, about 3 minutes. Remove the skillet from the heat and stir in the breadcrumbs and crabmeat.

In a large bowl mix together the eggs, salt, mustard and Worcestershire sauce. To this add the crab mixture and enough cream to hold the mixture together.

Shape the mixture into 12 cakes. Dredge the cakes in the flour.

Heat a ¼-inch layer of the olive oil in a large skillet. When hot add the crab cakes. Fry until golden brown, about 3 minutes a side. Serve with lemon wedges.

serves 4 to 6

❧ Soups and Salads ❧

As regularly as the tides come in, people make pilgrimages to the inns and restaurants of New England to taste the simple delights of traditional hearty soups and chowders. Always a mainstay of New England cooking, these robust soups were prepared in Colonial times in large, cast-iron pots that hung by the huge open hearth found in every New England kitchen. The aroma would fill the house from floorboards to rafters, whetting appetites for milky-white chowder filled with large chunks of fish, seafood and potatoes, or thick bean soup simmered with succulent pieces of pork.

Today, updated versions of these recipes retain the hearty, full-bodied taste and simplicity of preparation found in Colonial days. Soups like Fruit of the Sea Chowder, Home-Style Yankee Bean Soup and Portuguese Chorizo Soup can be meals in themselves—perfect for a weekend lunch, a light supper, or as an essential and delicious part of a New England feast.

New England salads tend to be hearty as well. Dishes like Lobster Salad and Fruit and Chicken Salad are meals for lunch or a light supper. Potato Salad, Spring Rice Salad and Marinated Bean Salad, among others, are traditional, delicious accompaniments to any main course.

❧ Boston Baked Bean Soup

2 cups cold baked beans
2 medium onions, chopped
1 small garlic clove, finely chopped
¼ teaspoon caraway seeds
4 cups water
2 cups canned tomatoes
2 tablespoons flour
2 tablespoons butter
salt to tast
freshly ground black pepper to taste

Put the beans, onions, garlic, caraway seeds and water into a large pot and simmer for 20 to 30 minutes.

Process the canned tomatoes in an electric blender or food processor at a low setting until they become a coarse purée. Pour the tomatoes into the bean mixture and continue to simmer gently.

Remove ¼ cup of the soup from the pot. Put it into a small bowl and mix in the flour and butter until a thin paste is formed. Pour this mixture back into the pot and simmer, stirring until the soup thickens to the desired consistency. Season with salt and pepper to taste.

serves 6

❧ Cabbage Soup

1 small head green cabbage, cored
3 boiling cups milk
1 cup light cream
salt to taste
freshly ground black pepper to taste
3 tablespoons butter

Chop the cabbage finely and place it in a large pot. Add enough boiling water to cover, and cook over moderate heat 7 minutes in an uncovered pot. Drain, reserving 1 cup of the cabbage stock.

To the cabbage add the milk, reserved cabbage stock and cream. Simmer for 3 minutes. Season to taste with salt and pepper.

Serve in large bowls, topped with the butter.

serves 4

❧ Codfish Chowder

3 pounds fresh codfish
3 onions, finely chopped
1 carrot
3 sprigs parsley
1 bay leaf
1 whole clove
1½ teaspoons salt
2 pounds potatoes
2 tablespoons butter
salt to taste
black pepper to taste
2 cups milk
1 tablespoon chopped parsley
½ cup shredded lettuce

Trim the skin and bones from the codfish and place the trimmings in a large pot. Add enough water to cover and add one-third of the onions and the carrot, parsley sprigs, bay leaf, salt and clove. Bring to a boil and cook for 15 minutes.

Dice the codfish fillets and the potatoes into small pieces about ½-inch square.

Melt the butter in a deep saucepan and sauté the remaining onions until lightly browned. Strain the fish broth over the onions. Add the diced codfish and potatoes. Simmer for 30 minutes, or until the potatoes are tender.

Add salt and pepper to taste and the milk, chopped parsley and lettuce. Heat thoroughly and serve at once.

serves 6

❧ Clam Chowder

1 quart hard-shelled clams
½ pound salt pork, diced
3 onions, finely chopped
2 cups boiling water
3 potatoes, finely diced
½ teaspoon freshly ground black pepper
3 cups milk
2 cups heavy cream
salt to taste

Scrub the clams and open them, reserving the juice. Chop the clams and save the juice.

Sauté the salt pork in large pot until it is light brown; pour off most of the fat. Add the onions and sauté until brown. Add the boiling water, potatoes, pepper, and clam juice. Cover and cook over medium heat for 20 minutes.

Add the clams, milk, and cream, stirring gently. Cook over low heat for 15 minutes, being careful not to let the soup boil. Season to taste with salt and black pepper.

The Indians had always made soup with clams, but it took the introduction of milk cows by the colonists to create true New England-style clam chowder. The word chowder comes from the French word *chaudrée*, meaning a thick fish soup cooked in a large *chaudron*, or cauldron.

serves 6 to 8

❧ Yankee Bean Chowder

1 cup dried pea beans or navy beans.
1 onion, finely chopped
1 cup diced carrots
1 green pepper, diced
1½ cups canned tomatoes
1 teaspoon salt
½ teaspoon freshly ground black pepper
1 cup diced potatoes
2 cups milk

On the day before cooking, wash and sort through the beans. Put them into a large bowl and add 3 cups cold water. Let soak overnight.

On cooking day, drain the beans and place in a large pot with 1½ quarts cold water. Add the onion and bring to a boil, then cover and simmer over low heat until the beans are tender, about 30 minutes.

Add the carrots, green pepper, tomatoes, salt and pepper into the pot and cook for 20 minutes, or until the beans have come apart and thickened the soup. (If you like a thick, purée-style soup, you can put the mixture in the blender, which will break up the beans.) Add the potatoes and milk and cook for 10 minutes longer, or until the potatoes are tender but not overly soft. Season to taste with additional salt and pepper.

serves 6

❧ Fruit of the Sea Chowder

12 oysters and their liquid
12 clams, steamed and shelled (reserve the liquid)
1 quart mussels, steamed and shelled
6 shrimp, cooked, shelled, and deveined
1 celery stalk, chopped
1 onion, finely chopped
2 leeks, finely chopped
¼ pound butter
3 cups milk
3 potatoes, diced
1 cup light cream
3 egg yolks

Poach the oysters in their liquid just until their edges curl; drain and reserve the liquid. Prepare the other shellfish as directed above and set aside.

In a medium saucepan, sauté the celery, onions, and leeks gently in the butter. Add

½ cup oysters, ½ cup clam liquid, ½ cup oyster liquid, milk and potatoes to the saucepan. Cook for 20 minutes, then press ingredients through a sieve and return them to the saucepan.

Place the egg yolks in a bowl and beat them. Heat the cream and pour it over the egg yolks, beating constantly. Add this mixture to the ingredients in the saucepan. Do not let boil.

Place the prepared shellfish in a soup tureen and pour the liquid over it.

serves 4

❧ Down-East Haddock Chowder

⅓ cup diced salt pork
1 onion, quartered and sliced
3 potatoes peeled and cubed
2 pounds haddock fillets, cut into cubes
1 quart water
1 small celery stalk with leaves, chopped
salt to taste
freshly ground black pepper to taste
⅛ teaspoon ground mace
2½ cups milk
½ cup heavy cream

Sauté the salt pork in a large pot until the pieces are crisp at the edges and tender. Remove the pieces and reserve.

In the pork fat left in the pot, sauté the onion until the pieces are translucent but not brown. Add the potatoes, fish, water, celery, salt, pepper and mace and bring to a boil. Reduce the heat and simmer for about 15 minutes, or until the potatoes are tender and the fish flaky.

Stir in the milk, cream and salt pork pieces and slowly bring back to a boil. Serve over crackers or toasted bread rounds.

serves 6

✂ Cream of Tomato Soup

3 large tomatoes, peeled, seeded, and chopped
4 cups chicken stock
1 bay leaf
2 cups heavy cream
salt to taste
freshly ground black pepper to taste

In a large pot, combine the chicken stock, bay leaf, and chopped tomatoes. Cover and simmer for 20 minutes.

Meanwhile, heat the cream in a saucepan. Add the warm cream to the pot and cook, stirring until the ingredients are well blended. Do not let the mixture boil. Season to taste with salt and pepper. Remove the bay leaf before serving.

serves 6

✂ Creamy Carrot Soup

½ cup chopped onion
6 tablespoons butter
2 cups thinly sliced carrots
1 teaspoon salt
3 cups chicken broth
¼ cup raw long-grain rice
1 cup milk
1 cup light cream

Heat the butter in a saucepan. Add the onions and sauté until lightly browned, about 5 to 7 minutes. Add the carrots and salt. Mix well to coat the carrots with the butter and onion mixture. Cover and simmer over low heat for 20 minutes. Stir and simmer for 1 hour. Stir occasionally.

Place the soup in the container of a blender or food processor. Blend until smooth. Return the soup to the saucepan. Stir in the milk and cream. Continue stirring until the soup is heated through. Remove from heat and serve.

serves 6

✂ Cream of Turnip Soup

1½ cups beef broth
10 small white turnips, peeled and coarsely grated
1 teaspoon salt
½ teaspoon black pepper
1 tablespoon flour
1 tablespoon butter
1 cup light cream

In a large pot combine the beef broth, turnips, salt and pepper. Cover and simmer for 15 minutes.

In a small saucepan, melt the butter. Stir in the flour and combine until well blended. Add the mixture to the soup. Stir until smooth and cook 2 minutes longer.

Remove the pot from the heat. Stir in the cream. Season to taste and serve hot.

serves 6

✂ Lentil Sausage Soup

1 pound fresh pork sausage links
4 medium parsnips, peeled and cubed
2 onions, chopped
1 garlic clove, minced
10 cups hot water
2 cups red or brown lentils
salt to taste
½ teaspoon dried marjoram leaves
1 1-pound can whole tomatoes
4 ounces Swiss cheese, shredded

Put the sausages into a large pot or Dutch oven with a thin layer of water. Cover and cook for 5 minutes over medium heat. Uncover and cook for 10 minutes more, turning often, until the sausages are deep brown. Drain the sausages on paper towels and cut them into large chunks. Pour off all but ¼ cup of the drippings in the pot.

Add the parsnips, onions and garlic to the drippings, and cook slowly, stirring often, until the parsnips are soft and the onions are brown. Stir in the water, lentils, salt and marjoram and bring the mixture to a rapid boil. Reduce heat and simmer gently for 30 minutes, or until the lentils are tender.

Add the tomatoes and their juice and the sausage chunks to the pot. Continue to simmer, covered, for about 4 hours, or until the lentils have broken up and thickened the soup to a hearty consistency. Serve over toasted slices of crusty bread, topped with the shredded Swiss cheese.

serves 8

✼ Oyster Stew

2 cups whole shelled oysters
4 cups milk, scalded
¼ cup butter
1½ teaspoons salt
¼ teaspoon freshly ground black pepper
¼ teaspoon ground nutmeg
¼ teaspoon ground ginger

Strain the oysters through a cheesecloth or fine wire strainer, catching the oyster juice in a large pot. Wash the oysters in cold water, carefully checking for grit and pieces of shell.

Bring the oyster juice slowly to a boil. Add the washed oysters, bring the juice back to the boil for 30 seconds, and then simmer until the edges of the oysters curl, about 3 to 4 minutes. Remove the oysters with a spoon and cut them into halves, or if they're large, quarters.

Add the milk, butter, salt, pepper, nutmeg and ginger to the simmering oyster juice, and stir until evenly blended. Return the oysters to the stew and cook for 5 minutes over low heat. Serve immediately.

serves 4

✼ Portuguese Chorizo Soup

1 pound chorizo or smoked garlic sausage
¼ cup olive oil
1 onion, finely chopped
1 garlic clove, finely chopped
3 medium potatoes, peeled and cubed
6 cups chicken broth
1 28-ounce can peeled plum tomatoes, drained and chopped
1 pound cooked white beans, drained
½ pound kale or spinach leaves, stems cut and shredded
¼ teaspoon hot red pepper flakes
salt to taste

Prick the sausages several times with a fork, then place in a saucepan. Add just enough water to cover the sausages and bring to a boil, then reduce the heat and simmer for 15 minutes. Drain the water, reserving ½ cup, and slice the sausages to bite-sized pieces.

Heat the olive oil in a large pot and sauté the onion and garlic until transparent and tender, but not brown. Add the potatoes and cook for 2 minutes, stirring constantly. Add the hot red pepper flakes, and continue to stir for 1 minute longer. Add the chicken broth and bring the mixture to a boil. Cover the pot and cook for 20 minutes, or until the potatoes are soft.

Mash the potatoes with a potato masher while they are in the soup. Add the tomatoes, beans and reserved sausage water. Bring the soup back to a boil, cover and cook for 20 minutes longer.

Add the spinach or kale leaves and the cut sausages to the soup. Add salt to taste, and cook for another 5 minutes, or until the kale or spinach has wilted.

serves 6

Green Peas and New Potatoes

Boston Baked Beans

Glazed Onions

❧ Pumpkin Soup

6 cups peeled and seeded pumpkin wedges (if
    pumpkin is out of season, use a 2½-pound
    can of pumpkin purée, but try for fresh
    pumpkin)
⅓ cup butter
1 onion, finely chopped
8 cups chicken broth
1 tablespoon honey
salt to taste
freshly ground black pepper to taste
½ teaspoon ground allspice
3 tablespoons flour
2 cups light cream
ground nutmeg

Melt half the butter in a large pot. Add the
onion and sauté until it is clear and tender,
but not brown.

Add the pumpkin, broth, honey, salt and
pepper and boil, stirring frequently, for
about 35 minutes or until the pumpkin is
extremely tender. If using canned pumpkin
purée, simmer gently for 10 minutes, stirring
frequently.

Purée the mixture in a blender or food processor (disregard this step if using canned
pumpkin purée), and add the allspice.

Return the mixture to the pot and heat.

Blend together the remaining butter and
flour and whisk into the simmering soup.
Stir in the cream and continue to simmer
until the soup reaches a rich, thick consistency. Serve with a dash of nutmeg in the
center of each bowl.

The pumpkin is a native North American
food. Indians of the Northeast were par-
ticularly fond of it, both baked and made
into soup.

serves 8 to 10

❧ Yankee Vegetable Soup

1 tablespoon butter or lard
½ pound lean beef, cubed
½ pound veal, cubed
1 large onion, chopped
1 green pepper, chopped
1 cup chopped potato
1 cup diced carrot
½ turnip, pared and chopped
4 cups water
⅓ cup chopped celery
¼ teaspoon dried thyme
1 bay leaf
½ teaspoon salt
¼ teaspoon freshly ground black pepper
2 cups fresh corn cut from the cob
1 cup chopped tomatoes

Heat the butter in a large saucepan. Add
the beef, veal, onion, and green pepper and
sauté until onion is golden brown.

Add the potatoes, carrots, and turnip and
cook 3 minutes longer. Add the water and
the celery, thyme, bay leaf, salt and pepper.
Cover and simmer for 4 hours.

Add the corn and cook 1 hour longer.
Remove the bay leaf and the meat. Stir in
the tomatoes and simmer 5 minutes longer.
Season to taste with additional salt and
pepper and serve.

serves 6

❧ Endive Salad

6 medium potatoes
2 or 3 heads endive
1 small stalk celery
Sour cream dressing:
½ cup white wine vinegar
salt to taste
freshly ground black pepper to taste
1 tablespoon butter
1 egg, beaten
¾ cup sour cream

Peel the potatoes and parboil them. When the potatoes are cool enough to handle, dice them. Dice the endive and the celery.

Combine the vinegar, salt, pepper, butter, egg, and sour cream in a saucepan. Bring to a boil and stir until mixture thickens.

Add the potatoes, endive, and celery and heat thoroughly. Stir gently and do not allow the ingredients to boil. Serve at room temperature.

serves 4 to 6

℀ Green Salad with Honey Dressing

1 head green leaf romaine lettuce
½ head red cabbage, shredded
1 cucumber, peeled and sliced
6 whole scallions, chopped
¼ cup diced celery
½ cup shredded carrots
1 garlic clove, finely minced
1 teaspoon diced oregano
salt to taste
freshly ground black pepper to taste
Honey Dressing:
½ cup safflower or peanut oil
¼ cup cider vinegar
¼ cup fresh lemon juice
¼ cup honey

Tear the lettuce leaves into small pieces and put them in a large salad bowl. Add the cabbage, cucumber, scallions, celery and carrots. Toss. Sprinkle the garlic, oregano, salt and pepper over the salad.

Mix the oil, vinegar, lemon juice and honey together in a small bowl. Stir until the dressing is well blended. (If the honey is cold or too thick to blend easily, thin it with a little warm water before adding it to the other ingredients.) Pour the dressing over the salad and toss.

serves 8

℀ Escarole Salad

2 red onions, thinly sliced
3 tablespoons cider vinegar
salt to taste
1 head escarole, chopped
3 tomatoes, seeded and chopped
1 cucumber, peeled and diced
1 green pepper, cored and chopped
10 radishes, sliced
1 cup Greek black olives
½ pound feta cheese, cut into small squares
Dressing:
¼ cup red wine vinegar
1 teaspoon dry mustard
1 teaspoon sugar
1 cup olive oil
salt to taste
freshly ground black pepper to taste

Put the onions and vinegar into a large salad bowl, add salt generously, and press the onions with a wooden spoon or potato masher. Set the mixture aside for 30 minutes.

Put the escarole and tomatoes into the bowl with the onion mixture and toss lightly. Add the cucumber, green pepper, radishes, olives and feta cheese.

Put the vinegar, mustard and sugar into a mixing bowl and stir vigorously. Add the oil, salt and pepper and stir well again. Just before serving, pour the dressing over the salad and toss.

serves 10

℀ Creamy Cole Slaw

1 medium-sized cabbage, cored and finely
  shredded
½ cup heavy cream, whipped
¼ to ½ cup sugar
½ cup vinegar
½ teaspoon salt
½ teaspoon black pepper

Place the shredded cabbage in a large bowl.

Beat the sugar into the whipped cream. Taste to test sweetness. Beat in the vinegar.

Pour this mixture over the shredded cabbage. Season with salt and pepper. Refrigerate until ready to serve.

serves 6 to 8

✸ Spinach and Marinated Mushroom Salad

1½ pounds fresh spinach
1 pound fresh white button mushrooms
3 large garlic cloves, crushed
1 bay leaf
½ teaspoon dried thyme
½ teaspoon crushed dried rosemary
½ teaspoon dried basil
¼ teaspoon salt
¼ teaspoon freshly ground black pepper
3 tablespoons fresh lemon juice
½ cup olive oil
½ cup cider vinegar

Rinse the spinach leaves well in cold water to remove all grit. Discard any tough stems and blemished leaves. Drain the leaves well and pat them dry with paper towels. Trim the stems from the mushrooms. Wipe the caps clean. Put them into a saucepan and add enough boiling water to cover them. Cover the pan and boil for 4 minutes. Drain the mushrooms well and put them into a large bowl.

Put the garlic, bay leaf, thyme, rosemary, basil, salt, pepper, lemon juice, olive oil and vinegar into a mixing bowl. Mix well. Pour the marinade mixture over the drained mushrooms and chill for 1 hour.

Put the spinach leaves into a large salad bowl. Toss chilled marinated mushrooms once or twice, then add them to the spinach leaves. Toss the salad vigorously and serve.

serves 8

✸ Dandelion and Lettuce Salad

1 pound young dandelion greens or arugala
1 head lettuce
4 onions, thinly sliced
2 tomatoes, diced
2 teaspoons salt
3 tablespoons olive oil
½ green pepper
2 hard-boiled eggs, chopped
¼ pound grated Swiss cheese
¼ teaspoon cayenne pepper
½ teaspoon black pepper
4 tablespoons vinegar

Wash and trim the dandelions. Coarsely chop the dandelions, lettuce and green pepper.

Mix the dandelions, lettuce and green pepper with the cheese in a bowl. Add the cayenne pepper, salt and pepper and mix again. Add the oil and vinegar and mix.

Add the tomatoes, onions and eggs to the bowl. Toss lightly and serve.

serves 4 to 6

✸ Marinated Vegetable Salad

1 small head cauliflower, broken into flowerettes
3 small white onions, quartered
1 pound small whole mushrooms
2 green peppers, thinly julienned
2 carrots, thinly julienned
1 cup cherry tomatoes
Marinade:
1 cup olive oil
1½ cups red wine vinegar
¼ cup sugar
1 teaspoon black pepper
2 teaspoons salt
1 garlic clove, crushed

Place all the vegetables except the cherry tomatoes in a large bowl and set aside.

To make the marinade, in a saucepan combine the olive oil, vinegar, sugar, salt, pepper and garlic. Bring the mixture to a boil. Remove from the heat and let cool slightly.

Pour the marinade over the vegetables. When the mixture is cool, add the cherry tomatoes.

Refrigerate for a day, stirring often, before serving.

serves 6 to 8

Marinated Bean Salad

2 cups cooked baby lima beans
2 cups cooked green beans
3 cups cooked kidney beans
1 cup sliced cooked mushrooms
½ cup diced pimento
½ cup finely chopped scallion
2 tablespoons chopped parsley
½ cup red wine vinegar
½ cup olive oil
⅓ cup water
1 tablespoon honey
1 garlic clove, crushed
½ teaspoon dried oregano
¼ teaspoon celery salt
½ teaspoon salt
½ teaspoon freshly ground black pepper

Put the lima beans, green beans and kidney beans into a very large serving bowl. Add the mushrooms.

Combine the pimento, scallion, parsley, vinegar, olive oil, water, honey, garlic, oregano, celery salt, salt and pepper in a mixing bowl. Stir until well blended. Pour the dressing over the beans and mushrooms and toss vigorously. Cover the bowl and chill overnight. Toss again before serving.

serves 12

Spring Rice Salad

3 cups cooked long-grain rice
1 cup cooked wild rice
½ cup mayonnaise
¾ cup unflavored yogurt
1 cup chopped celery
2 tomatoes, seeded and diced
½ cup diced cucumber
¼ cup chopped parsley
1 small onion, chopped
salt to taste
freshly ground black pepper to taste

Do not use oil or butter when cooking the rices. Drain them well and let cool.

Put the long-grain rice and the wild rice into a large serving bowl. Add the mayonnaise, yogurt, celery, tomatoes, cucumber, parsley, onion and salt and pepper to taste. Toss well. Chill for 1 hour and serve.

serves 6

Potato Salad

½ cup French dressing
4 cps diced cooked potatoes
1 cup sour cream
3 whole scallions, chopped
2 tablespoons chopped parsley
½ dill pickle, chopped
2 tablespoons diced pimento
2 tablespoons cider vinegar
1 tablespoon Dijon-style mustard
4 hard-boiled eggs, finely chopped
1 teaspoon salt
freshly ground black pepper to taste
1 cup chopped celery

Put the potatoes in a large serving bowl, add the French dressing and toss lightly until the dressing coats the potatoes.

Put the sour cream into a small mixing bowl and add the scallions, parsley, pickle, pimento, vinegar, mustard, chopped eggs, salt and pepper. Stir until the ingredients are well mixed. Add the mixture to the potatoes. Add the celery to the potatoes. Toss well.

Chill for 1 hour and serve.

serves 6

✼ Carrot Salad

1 pound fresh carrots, washed and scraped
⅓ cup parsley, chopped
¼ cup scallion, chopped
½ teaspoon minced garlic
3 tablespoons olive oil
2 tablespoons fresh lemon juice
2 tablespoons honey
salt to taste
freshly ground black pepper to taste

Shred the carrots finely with a grater or food processor. There should be 4 to 6 cups. Put the carrots into a salad bowl and add the parsley, scallion and garlic.

Add the olive oil, lemon juice and honey and toss well. Season with salt and pepper to taste. Chill for 1 hour before serving.

serves 6

✼ Fruit and Chicken Salad

4 cups diced cooked chicken
1 cup diced celery
1 cup drained canned mandarin orange sections
1 cup seedless white grapes
1 cup drained canned pineapple chunks
3 tablespoons peanut oil
2 tablespoons fresh orange juice
2 tablespoons fresh lemon juice
1 teaspoon mayonnaise

In a large salad bowl, mix the chicken, celery, orange sections, grapes and pineapple chunks together.

In a smaller bowl, blend the peanut oil, orange juice and lemon juice together. Add to the chicken mixture and toss vigorously.

Chill the salad for 1 hour. Drain the liquid from salad into a mixing bowl. Whisk mayonnaise into the liquid to thicken it. Pour the dressing over the salad and toss.

serves 6

✼ Lobster Salad

3 cups cooked lobster meat, cut into bite-sized pieces
1 cup diced celery
1 whole scallion, chopped
1 teaspoon salt
¼ teaspoon paprika
2 tablespoons French dressing
1 tablespoon olive oil
4 pimento-stuffed green olives, sliced
lettuce leaves
1 hard-boiled egg, sliced
capers

Put the lobster meat, celery, scallion, salt, paprika, French dressing, olive oil and sliced olives in a bowl and mix until the ingredients are well-blended.

Arrange the lettuce leaves on a serving platter. Spoon the lobster salad onto the lettuce and garnish with slices of hard-boiled egg and capers.

serves 6

❧ Vegetables ❧

The first settlers in the New World discovered a wealth of new foods unknown in the Old World. Squash, pumpkin, green peppers, potatoes, corn, sweet potatoes, maple sugar, tomatoes—all were revelations. Some were slow to gain acceptance. The potato, a staple food the world over now, didn't gain wide-spread acceptance until the late seventeenth century. The tomato at first was grown as an ornamental plant; until into this century some people thought it was poisonous.

But from the very first, the earliest New England settlers learned from the Indians to eat the native foods. Corn was among the first of their crops. And ever since then, vegetable cookery has been an important part of their cooking.

In this chapter you'll find recipes for dishes that are a part of classic American cuisine. There's the dish that made Boston famous—Baked Beans—but there are also recipes that show there's more than one way to bake a bean, and more than one kind of bean to bake. A recipe for Succotash, a dish that is a direct gift from the Indians, is included, as well as unusual recipes for such New England delicacies as fiddlehead ferns.

❧ Fried Asparagus

12 fresh medium-sized asparagus spears
1 egg, beaten
¼ cup heavy cream
3 tablespoons flour
salt to taste
freshly ground black pepper to taste
4 tablespoons butter
¼ cup olive oil

Wash and trim the asparagus. Discard the tough ends.

Place the asparagus in a pot with enough lightly salted boiling water to cover. Cook for about 3 minutes, until just barely tender. Cool quickly under cold water, drain, and dry on paper towels.

Slice the spears thinly.

In a mixing bowl combine the egg and cream. Work in enough flour to make a semi-thick batter; season to taste with salt and pepper.

Dip the asparagus slices into the batter.

Heat the butter and oil in a skillet. Drop the asparagus by tablespoons into the skillet, in batches if necessary, and fry until golden on both sides. Drain on paper towels.

serves 4

❧ Boston Baked Beans

4 cups dried pea beans
1 medium-sized onion
½ pound salt pork
½ cup dark brown sugar, firmly packed
⅓ cup molasses
1 tablespoon salt
1 teaspoon dry mustard

Soak the beans overnight in 12 cups of cold water. Drain the beans well and place them in a large pot. Cover with cold water and slowly bring to a boil. Simmer until the beans are tender, about 1 hour or longer. Test for doneness by scooping up a few beans in a spoon and blowing on them. If the skins blow off, the beans are done.

Drain the beans and place 1 cup in a bean pot, heavy casserole or iron pot. Add the onion and cover it with the remaining beans. Score the salt pork to the rind and push it down among the beans until it just shows through the top.

Combine the brown sugar, molasses, salt and dry mustard in a small bowl. Pour the mixture over the beans and mix gently. Add enough hot water to fill the pot. The pork should protrude a little above the water line so that it can brown nicely.

Bake the beans in a 300° oven for at least 8 hours. The juice should bubble at the top of the pot all day. Add more water if necessary during baking. Check the beans every hour or so. Serve in the pot.

serves 6 to 8

❧ Boiled Beans Bake

4 cups dried pea or yelloweye beans
8 cups water
1 cup beef broth
½ cup pure maple syrup
2 onions, chopped
1 tablespoon salt
1 teaspoon freshly ground black pepper
3 beef marrow bones
½ pound salt pork or bacon, sliced

Soak the beans overnight in 12 cups cold water. Drain well and place the beans in a large pot. Cover with water and simmer until tender, about 1 hour or longer. Add more water if necessary. When the beans are tender, add the beef broth, maple syrup, onions, salt and pepper.

Place the marrow bones in a bean pot, heavy casserole or iron pot. Add the bean mixture. Cover the beans with the slices of salt pork. Cover the pot and bake in 250° oven for 4 to 6 hours. Check the beans every hour; add more broth if necessary.

serves 8 to 10

❧ Maple Baked Beans

1 pound dried pea beans
2 teaspoons dry mustard
freshly ground black pepper to taste
1 cup pure maple syrup
6 strips salt pork or Canadian bacon
1 onion, peeled

In a large pot, cover the beans with cold water and soak them for 8 hours.

After soaking, heat the beans to a rapid boil, then reduce the heat, cover and gently simmer for about 1 hour, or until the beans are firm but tender.

Drain the beans and reserve the stock.

Put three salt pork or bacon strips on the bottom of a large, deep casserole or baking dish (at least 3 quarts). Pour in the beans, and add the mustard, pepper and maple syrup. Stir thoroughly until the ingredients are well mixed. Bury the onion deep in the beans, and lay the three remaining strips of salt pork or bacon on top.

Pour the reserved bean stock into the beans until the liquid rises to a level just below the surface.

Cover the pot and bake at 275° for about 6 hours. Add more stock as needed.

After 6 hours, uncover the pot and bake for another hour, until the beans are soft and bubbly.

This dish is similar in spirit to a favorite Indian dish.

serves 8 to 10

❧ Harvard Beets

12 small fresh beets
½ cup sugar
2 teaspoons cornstarch
½ cup red or white wine vinegar
2 tablespoons butter

Cut the tops from the beets, leaving 1 inch of stem. Wash the beets and place them in a saucepan with enough cold water to cover. Bring to a boil. When the water begins to boil, cover the saucepan and reduce the heat. Simmer until the beets are tender. Test the beets often with a fork; avoid overcooking them.

When the beets are done, drain them well. When they are cool enough to handle, peel the beets (skins should slip off easily). Cut them into slices or julienne strips and place them in a large saucepan.

Combine the sugar, cornstarch and vinegar in a small saucepan. Bring to a boil and simmer for 4 to 5 minutes. Pour the mixture over the beets. Stir gently and heat very slowly over low heat. Shake the saucepan often. Just before serving the beets, add the butter and let it melt into the sauce.

serves 6

✂ Broccoli Cheddar Casserole

2 large bunches broccoli, about 2 pounds
20 small white onions
salt to taste
4 tablespoons butter
4 tablespoons flour
1½ cups milk
¾ cup light cream
2 cups grated sharp Vermont cheddar cheese
freshly ground black pepper to taste

Cut off the bottom of the broccoli stems where they start to become woody, about 1 to 1½ inches from the bottom.

Fill a large pot with cold water to a depth of 1 inch. Stand the broccoli stem down in the pot. Cover the pot tightly, and steam the broccoli over very high heat until they are bright green and crisp-tender, about 5 to 6 minutes.

Peel and halve the onions. Put the onions in a saucepan and add enough water to cover. Add a little salt and cook slowly, uncovered, until the onions are slightly soft.

Melt the butter in a saucepan and whisk in the flour a little at a time. When smooth, add the milk while stirring rapidly with the whisk. When the sauce begins to thicken, add the cream and simmer over low heat for 5 minutes. Do not let the sauce boil. Remove the saucepan from the heat. Stir in 1 cup of the cheese, using a wooden spoon, until the cheese is blended. Season the cheese with salt and pepper to taste.

Preheat the oven to 350°

Drain the broccoli and cut them into bite-sized pieces.

Butter a large casserole dish. Put alternate layers of broccoli and onions in it, and top them with the cheese sauce. Spread the remaining grated cheddar on top and bake for 1 hour, or until the cheese is browned on top.

serves 4 to 6

✂ Corn Pudding

2 cups cooked corn
2 whole scallions, chopped
3 eggs, beaten
3 tablespoons melted butter
1 cup milk
1 cup light cream
1½ teaspoons salt
freshly ground black pepper to taste
¼ pound Virginia ham, chopped

Combine all the ingredients in a mixing bowl. Butter a large (at least 2 quarts) casserole or baking dish. Spread the mixture evenly in the dish.

Preheat the oven to 325°

Set the casserole or baking dish in the center of a roasting pan. Add enough water to the pan so that it comes halfway up the sides of the casserole or baking dish.

Bake about 1 hour, or until the top is nicely browned and the pudding is firm.

serves 6

❁ Corn Fritters

2 eggs, separated
2 cups fresh corn kernels, cut from the cob
2 tablespoons sugar
½ teaspoon salt
1 slice stale bread, crumbled
butter

In a mixing bowl combine the egg yolks, corn kernels, sugar, salt and bread crumbs.

In another bowl, beat the egg whites until they are stiff but not dry. Carefully fold the corn mixture into the egg whites.

Heat a griddle or skillet. Add enough butter to fry the fritters. When the butter has melted, add the fritters. Form the fritters by molding a tablespoon of the batter gently in your hands. Fry one side at a time until golden brown. Add additional butter as needed. Serve immediately.

serves 4

❁ Butter-Fried Dandelion Flowers

4 cups fresh, wild dandelion flowers
½ cup butter
2 eggs, lightly beaten
flour
salt to taste
freshly ground black pepper to taste

Make sure your dandelion flowers have not been contaminated by fertilizer, weed killers, or pets. Do not wash the dandelions. This will make them close up. Pick over the flowers to clean them of any dirt, then pat them lightly with a wet paper towel.

Melt the butter in a large skillet over a medium heat.

Dip each flower in the beaten eggs, then in the flour and fry quickly in the skillet until golden brown.

Season the hot dandelion flowers with a sprinkling of salt and pepper, and serve piping hot.

serves 6

❁ Braised Fiddlehead Ferns

1 pound fresh or frozen fiddlehead ferns
2 cups water
1 tablespoon lemon juice
2 tablespoons butter
½ teaspoon salt

Remove the fuzz from the fiddleheads. Rinse them well in cold water. If using frozen fiddleheads, thaw them first.

In a large skillet, bring the water to a boil. Drop in the fiddleheads and simmer, uncovered, until tender, about 30 minutes for fresh fiddleheads and less for frozen.

Drain the water well leaving the fiddleheads in the skillet. Add the lemon juice, butter and salt. Shake the skillet to distribute the butter and salt. Serve warm.

Fiddlehead ferns grow wild in New England in the very early spring. Frozen fiddleheads are often found in well-stocked supermarkets.

serves 4

✺ Stuffed Mushrooms

24 large white mushrooms
2 garlic cloves, minced
¼ pound butter
1 cup unflavored bread crumbs
½ teaspoon salt
¼ teaspoon freshly ground black pepper
¼ teaspoon ground dried sage
2 tablespoons chopped parsley
½ cup grated Romano cheese

Carefully loosen and remove the stems from the mushroom caps. Set the caps aside and chop the stems.

Melt 4 tablespoons of butter in a skillet and sauté the chopped mushroom stems with the bread crumbs, salt, pepper, sage and parsley.

Remove the stuffing from the skillet, and sauté the mushroom caps over low heat in 3 tablespoons butter until their surface is glazed and slightly browned, about 2 minutes.

Fill the mushroom caps with the stuffing. Melt the remaining butter and drizzle it over all the caps. Top each cap with the grated Romano cheese.

Place the mushrooms in a baking dish, and bake at 350° for about 15 minutes.

serves 6

✺ Fried Mushrooms

1 pound fresh small mushrooms
1 egg, beaten
unflavored bread crumbs
salt to taste
olive oil

Wipe the mushrooms clean with damp paper towels.

Dip the mushrooms in the beaten egg and then in the bread crumbs.

Place the oil in a deep skillet and heat it to 375°. Add the mushrooms and fry until they are browned. Drain on paper towels. Season with salt before serving.

serves 4 to 6

✺ Onions in Cream Sauce

24 small white onions
2 tablespoons butter
2 tablespoons flour
½ cup milk
½ cup heavy cream
salt to taste
¼ cup chopped parsley

Peel the onions. Place them in a saucepan with enough cold salted water to cover and bring to a boil. Reduce the heat and cook slowly until the onions are tender when tested with a fork. Drain well.

Melt the butter in a saucepan and add the flour, a little at a time. Stir constantly until the sauce is smooth, and simmer gently over low heat for 3 minutes longer.

Stir in the milk and cream and continue cooking, stirring constantly, until the sauce is thickened and smooth. Do not let the sauce boil. Remove the sauce from the heat and stir in the salt and parsley. Pour the sauce over the onions and serve hot.

serves 4

✺ Glazed Onions

10 medium-sized onions
10 teaspoons honey
4 tablespoons butter
salt to taste
freshly ground black pepper to taste

Preheat the oven to 450°.

Cut the onions in half horizontally. Butter each onion and arrange them in a buttered baking dish, cut-side up. Sprinkle the onions with salt and pepper to taste.

Pour 1 teaspoon honey over each onion. Dot with butter. Bake, uncovered, for 45 minutes.

serves 4 to 5

Glazed Parsnips

2 pounds parsnips
½ cup butter
salt to taste
½ cup pure maple syrup

Wash the parsnips. Place them in a saucepan and cover them with cold water. Bring the water to a boil and cook until the parsnips are tender when tested with a fork.

Remove the parsnips from water and drain well. When cool enough to handle, peel, halve, and remove the cores.

Melt the butter in a skillet. Add the parsnips and sprinkle them lightly with salt. Add the maple syrup. Cook, turning once, until the parsnips are slightly browned and glazed.

serves 6

Glazed Baby Carrots

2 pounds baby carrots, trimmed
6 tablespoons butter
6 tablespoons sugar
½ teaspoon ground ginger

Place just enough salted water in a saucepan to cover the carrots. bring to a boil and add the carrots. Cook for 12 to 15 minutes or until carrots are tender. Drain well.

In a skillet, combine the butter, sugar and ginger. Cook, stirring constantly, until well blended. Add the carrots and continue cooking over low heat. Shake the skillet frequently. Make sure the carrots are thoroughly glazed on all sides. Remove from the heat and serve hot.

serves 4 to 6

Baked Cabbage

1 medium-sized cabbage, cored and cut into eighths
boiling water
3 tablespoons melted butter
4 tablespoons cider vinegar
1 teaspoon salt
½ teaspoon black pepper

Preheat the oven to 325°.

Place the cabbage pieces into a large pot and cover them with boiling water. Cook over medium heat for 15 minutes or until tender. Drain well and cool.

Chop the cabbage finely and place it in a large mixing bowl. Add the melted butter, cider vinegar, salt and pepper. Mix well.

Turn mixture into a buttered baking dish and bake for 20 to 30 minutes. Remove from oven and serve hot.

serves 4

Braised Celery

2 large red onions, very thinly sliced
salt to taste
black pepper to taste
¼ cup butter
4 cups celery, cut diagonally into ½-inch slices
2 cups beef broth
2 tablespoons water
1 tablespoon cornstarch

Preheat the oven to 325°.

Arrange the onion slices in a buttered 1½-quart casserole dish. Season with the salt and pepper.

In a skillet, heat the butter. Add the celery and cook over moderate heat until lightly browned, about 5 minutes. Stir often.

Heat the beef broth in a saucepan.

Combine the cornstarch and water in a small bowl. Blend until smooth. Add the mixture to the broth. Bring the broth to a boil and cook, stirring constantly, for 3 to 5 minutes or until the sauce is thick and smooth.

Add the sauce to the celery and mix well. Spoon the mixture over the onions in the casserole dish. Bake for 1 hour. Serve hot.

serves 6

❧ Spinach with Rosemary

2 pounds fresh spinach
¼ teaspoon fresh rosemary or ½ teaspoon dried
1 scallion, chopped (including green part)
2 tablespoons butter
salt to taste
freshly ground black pepper to taste

Wash the spinach carefully to remove all grit. Remove any tough stems and blemished leaves.

Chop the spinach coarsely and place it in a large saucepan with the rosemary, scallion, butter, salt and pepper. Cook, covered, for about 5 minutes or until the spinach is limp but still bright green. Do not add any water to the saucepan; the spinach will cook in its own juices.

serves 4

❧ Green Peas and New Potatoes

¼ pound sliced salt pork or bacon
2 small onions, chopped
8 small new potatoes
2 cups cooked peas
1 cup heavy cream

In a small skillet fry the pork or bacon slices until crisp. Remove meat from skillet and add onions. Cook until lightly browned.

Scrub but do not peel the potatoes. Place them in a saucepan, add the pork or bacon, the onions and just enough cold water to cover. Cook over moderate heat, covered, for 20 minutes.

Remove the pork or bacon slices. Add the peas to the potatoes and onions. Pour the cream over the vegetables and simmer until well blended. Do not let the cream boil.

This dish is traditionally served with poached salmon on the Fourth of July.

serves 4

❧ Parsnip Fritters

5 parsnips
1 tablespoon butter
1 tablespoon flour
1 egg, beaten
peanut or vegetable oil
salt to taste
freshly ground black pepper to taste

Put the parsnips in a large pot and add enough cold water to cover them. Bring to a boil and cook until the parsnips are very soft. Drain the parsnips. When they are cool enough to handle, peel them and put them into a large mixing bowl. Mash the parsnips thoroughly. Add salt to taste and beat in the butter, flour and egg. Season with pepper to taste and a little more salt.

Shape the mixture into small round cakes.

Heat a thin layer of vegetable or peanut oil in a skillet. When the oil is very hot, drop in the fritters, leaving room between them. Cook the fritters in batches if necessary. Turn the fritters carefully with a spatula, and cook them both sides until they are a deep golden brown.

Drain the fritters on paper towels. Keep them warm while the other fritters are cooking. Serve with applesauce.

serves 4

✄ Pease Porridge

1 pound dried split green peas
1 teaspoon salt
1 onion, quartered
¼ teaspoon ground cloves
½ teaspoon dried marjoram
½ teaspoon dried tarragon
freshly ground black pepper to taste
3 tablespoons butter

Rinse and pick over the peas. Drain well.

Put the peas in a large pot and cover with cold water. Bring to a boil, and add the salt, onion and cloves. Reduce the heat to low and simmer for 1 hour, stirring occasionally and adding more water as necessary.

Add the marjoram, tarragon and pepper and slowly simmer for another hour. Stir every 10 minutes to prevent the peas from sticking.

When the pea mixture is very, very thick, push it through a sieve or coarsely purée it in a blender or food processor. Season to taste with additional salt and pepper and serve dotted with butter.

serves 8

✄ Hubbard Squash Pie

2 cups cooked mashed Hubbard squash
¾ cup firmly packed light brown sugar
¾ teaspoon cinnamon
½ teaspoon grated nutmeg
¼ teaspoon ground ginger
½ teaspoon salt
3 tablespoons melted butter
1 tablespoon molasses
2 eggs, beaten
2 cups scalded milk
pastry for 1 9-inch pie crust

Preheat the oven to 450°.

In a large mixing bowl combine the Hubbard squash, sugar, cinnamon, nutmeg, ginger, salt, melted butter, molasses, eggs and milk. Blend thoroughly. Turn the mixture into a 9-inch pie lined with the pastry.

Bake for 20 minutes. Reduce heat to 350° and bake for 35 minutes longer or until the filling is firm to the touch.

✄ Jerusalem Artichokes

1½ pounds Jerusalem artichokes
½ cup melted butter
3 tablespoons lemon juice
½ teaspoon salt
¼ teaspoon black pepper

Peel and trim the Jerusalem artichokes. Place them in a saucepan filled with boiling salted water and cook until tender, approximately 15 minutes. Test often with a fork as the artichokes cook; do not overcook them.

Remove the artichokes from the water and drain thoroughly.

In a bowl combine the melted butter, lemon juice, salt and pepper. Pour over artichokes and toss lightly.

serves 4 to 6

❧ Potatoes with Mustard Sauce

4 large new potatoes
6 tablespoons butter
1 small onion, chopped
3 tablespoons sifted flour
2 cups chicken broth
1 cup light cream
4 tablespoons Dijon-style mustard
salt to taste
freshly ground black pepper to taste
bread crumbs
grated Parmesan cheese

Scrub the potatoes and cut them into
½-inch slices. Put the slices into a large pot
of boiling salted water. Reduce the heat and
simmer the potatoes for about 30 minutes.

While the potatoes simmer, melt half the
butter in a saucepan. Add the onion and
sauté until transparent but not browned.
Stir in the sifted flour, broth and cream.
Continue to stir slowly until evenly blended.
Raise the heat slightly, until the mixture
begins to boil, and stir in the mustard.
When the mustard is fully blended into the
sauce, remove the saucepan from the heat
and keep it warm by placing the pan over a
pot of simmering water.

Preheat the oven to 375°.

Drain the potatoes and spread them in
layers in a casserole dish, seasoning each
layer with a light dusting of salt and pepper.

Pour the sauce over the potatoes. Sprinkle
the bread crumbs and Parmesan cheese
generously on top. Dot with pieces of the
remaining butter, and bake, uncovered, until
lightly browned and bubbly.

serves 6

❧ Hashed Brown Potatoes

2 cups cold baked potatoes, skinned and
    chopped
1 small onion, chopped
salt to taste
freshly ground black pepper to taste
⅓ cup salt pork fat, butter, or bacon fat

Combine the potatoes, onion, salt and
pepper in a mixing bowl. Mix gently.

Heat the fat in a skillet. When it is very hot,
add the potato mixture. Cook for 3 minutes,
stirring constantly.

Reduce the heat and cook until the potatoes
are brown and crisp on the bottom. Fold
the potatoes over and serve.

serves 4

❧ Potato and Turnip Bake

3 large baking potatoes
2 cups mashed cooked turnip
3 tablespoons butter
hot milk
salt to taste
freshly ground black pepper to taste

Preheat the oven to 450°

Scrub the potatoes and bake them for 45
minutes or until done.

When the potatoes are done, cut them into
halves lengthwise and scoop out the pulp.
Save the shells and put the pulp into a
bowl. Add the turnip and butter to the
bowl and mix well. Beat in enough hot milk
to make the mixture light and fluffy. Season
with salt and pepper to taste.

Fill the reserved potato shells with the mixture and place in the oven to brown lightly.

serves 6

✳ Potato Croquettes

1½ cups cold mashed potatoes
1 tablespoon melted butter
1 teaspoon chopped parsley
2 tablespoons light cream
¼ teaspoon salt
½ teaspoon chopped onion
⅛ teaspoon cayenne pepper
1 egg, separated
olive oil or butter
breadcrumbs

Combine the potatoes and butter in a mixing bowl. Mix into a paste. Add the parsley, salt, cayenne, cream, onion and egg yolk.

Shape the mixture into small patties or croquettes. Dip the patties into the beaten egg white, then roll them in the breadcrumbs to coat.

Heat the oil or butter in a skillet. Fry the croquettes until golden brown on both sides. Add additional oil as needed. Serve hot.

serves 4

✳ Acorn Squash with Rum Butter Glaze

4 large acorn squash
½ cup butter
⅔ cup water
½ cup light rum
1 cup firmly packed dark brown sugar
rind of 1 large orange, grated

Preheat the oven to 350°. Trim the ends from the squash. Cut each squash into 4 rings. Remove the seeds.

Place the rings side-by-side in 2 buttered shallow baking pans. Add ⅓ cup water to each pan. Cover the pans with aluminum foil and bake for 40 to 45 minutes or until the squash rings are almost tender. Remove the foil.

Melt the butter in a saucepan. Add the rum, brown sugar, and orange rind and stir well. Pour one-quarter of the mixture into each pan. Lift the squash rings to allow the liquid to run underneath. Bake, uncovered, for another 10 minutes. Turn the rings and pour the remaining butter-rum mixture over them. Bake another 10 minutes. Serve the rings on a platter with the pan juices poured over them.

serves 6 to 8

✳ Stuffed Acorn Squash

3 acorn squash
1 cup unsweetened applesauce
⅓ cup firmly packed light brown sugar
1 tablespoon lemon juice
⅓ cup mixed dark and light seedless raisins
¼ cup coarsely chopped walnuts
2 tablespoons butter
hot water

Preheat the oven to 400°.

Cut each squash in half lengthwise. Remove the seeds and stringy pulp.

In a mixing bowl combine the applesauce, brown sugar, lemon juice, raisins and walnuts. Spoon the mixture into the squash halves. Place the squash in a baking dish and add enough hot water to cover the bottom of the dish to a depth of ½ inch. Dot the squash with butter.

Cover the dish and bake for 25 minutes. Remove the cover and bake 30 minutes longer, or until the squash are tender.

serves 6

❆ Summer Squash Casserole

3 cups coarsely chopped zucchini and/or yellow
    summer squash
½ teaspoon salt
¼ teaspoon black pepper
3 tablespoons butter
½ cup sour cream
1 small onion, finely chopped
2 eggs, beaten
¼ teaspoon grated nutmeg
¼ teaspoon crushed hot red pepper flakes
2 cups unflavored breadcrumbs

Preheat the oven to 350°.

Steam the squash until tender, about 3 to 5
minutes. drain well and place the squash in
a mixing bowl. season with the salt, pepper
and butter. Add the sour cream, onion,
eggs, nutmeg and red pepper flakes. Mix
well.

Lightly butter a 1½-quart casserole dish.
Place a layer of half the squash mixture into
the dish. Top with 1 cup of the breadcrumbs. Then add the rest of the squash
mixture and top with the remaining breadcrumbs.

Bake, uncovered, for 30 minutes. Serve hot.

serves 6 to 8

❆ Rice and Spinach Casserole

3 cups cooked rice
1 cup chopped spinach
2 eggs, beaten
1 cup milk
1 teaspoon Worcestershire sauce
1¼ teaspoons salt
2 teaspoons chopped onions
¼ cup butter
½ cup grated sharp Cheddar cheese

Preheat the oven to 325°.

In a large mixing bowl combine the rice and
spinach. Add the eggs, milk, Worcestershire
sauce, salt and onions. Combine gently.

Place the mixture in a buttered 2-quart baking dish. Dot with the butter and sprinkle
with the cheese. Bake for 30 to 40 minutes
or until the casserole is heated through and
the cheese is golden.

serves 4 to 6

❆ Succotash

3 tablespoons butter
2 cups cooked lima beans
2 cups corn, fresh, canned, or frozen
½ cup water
1 teaspoon salt
1 teaspoon sugar
½ teaspoon pepper
¼ cup light cream

Melt the butter in a saucepan. Add the lima
beans and the corn. (If using fresh corn,
cook it first.) Toss lightly until coated with
butter.

Add the water, salt, sugar and pepper. Cover
and cook over low heat until the water is
absorbed.

Stir in the cream. Cook the succotash over
low heat until the cream is thoroughly
heated. Serve hot.

The Narragansett Indians taught the
Pilgrims how to make succotash. The dish
was served at the first Thanksgiving dinner.

serves 4

Stuffed Clams

Lobster Salad

Succotash

Marinated Bean Salad

New England Boiled Dinner

Shrimp and Corn Soufflé

Cranberry-Stuffed Mackerel

Boiled Lobster

❧ Sweet Potatoes and Cranberries

6 large sweet potatoes
2 cups whole fresh cranberries
2 cups water
1 cup brown sugar
¼ cup honey
1 teaspoon grated orange rind
¾ teaspoon cinnamon
1½ tablespoons butter

Peel the sweet potatoes and cut them in half lengthwise.

Put the potatoes in a pot and cover them with cold water. Bring the water to a boil, then reduce the heat and simmer until the sweet potatoes are tender when tested with a fork.

Put the cranberries in a large saucepan and add 2 cups water. Cook the cranberries over a high heat for 10 minutes, or until they pop open. Reduce the heat and add the brown sugar, honey, orange rind and cinnamon. Simmer for another 10 minutes, stirring constantly, until the sauce thickens.

Preheat the oven to 300°.

Raise the heat a little, add the butter and continue to simmer and stir until the butter melts and blends into the sauce.

Put the sweet potatoes in a baking dish. Pour the sauce over the potatoes and bake for 20 minutes.

serves 6

❧ Sweet Potato Casserole

6 parboiled sweet potatoes, peeled and halved
2 cups apples, peeled, cored, and thinly sliced
½ cup pure maple syrup
½ teaspoon salt
1 tablespoon lemon juice
3 tablespoons butter

Preheat the oven to 350°.

In a buttered, 1-quart baking dish, arrange layers of the sweet potato and apple.

In a bowl, combine the maple syrup, salt, and lemon juice. Pour over the sweet potato mixture in the baking dish. Dot with butter and bake for 45 minutes.

serves 6

❧ Scalloped Tomatoes

½ cup butter
1 medium-sized onion, chopped
2 cups chopped fresh or canned tomatoes
1 teaspoon salt
1 tablespoon sugar
½ teaspoon freshly ground black pepper
2 cups unflavored bread crumbs

Preheat the oven to 375°.

In a skillet melt 2 tablespoons of the butter. Add the chopped onion and cook until it is translucent but not brown.

In a mixing bowl combine the onions, tomatoes, salt, sugar and pepper.

Butter a medium-sized baking dish. Place a layer of the tomato mixture in the dish, followed by a layer of bread crumbs. Repeat, alternating layers and ending with a layer of crumbs. Dot the top with the remaining butter. Bake for 30 to 40 minutes, or until bubbly and browned on top.

serves 4 to 6

✂ Pan-Fried Tomatoes

3 large, firm tomatoes
¼ cup flour
¼ cup butter
salt to taste
freshly ground black pepper to taste

Cut the tomatoes into ½-inch slices. Do not peel.

Place the flour in a small bowl and dip the tomato slices into it.

Melt the butter in a skillet and add the tomatoes. Sauté until the slices are browned on both sides. Sprinkle with salt and pepper and serve.

serves 4

✂ Braised Turnips

1½ pounds turnips, peeled and cut into
    matchsticks
½ cup butter
⅓ cup beef broth
1 tablespoon lemon juice
3 tablespoons chopped parsley
salt to taste
freshly ground black pepper to taste

Sauté the turnip matchsticks in the butter in a large skillet, stirring occasionally, for 3 minutes. Stir in the beef broth and lemon juice. Braise the turnips, covered, over low heat for 8 minutes, or until they are tender. Stir in the parsley and salt and pepper to taste.

serves 6

✂ Casserole-Baked Zucchini

vegetable oil
6 small zucchini, thinly sliced
1 teaspoon salt
½ teaspoon freshly ground black pepper
4 eggs, beaten
1½ cups milk
1 tablespoon flour
¼ teaspoon cayenne pepper
½ cup grated Swiss cheese

Pour a thin layer of vegetable oil into a saucepan, add the sliced zucchini and cook over very low heat, stirring frequently, until the zucchini is soft, but still bright green, about 4 minutes.

Preheat the oven to 400°.

Combine the eggs, milk, flour and cayenne pepper in a mixing bowl and mix together with a slotted spoon or wire whisk. Beat the mixture thoroughly, until it starts to froth.

Drain the zucchini, add to the mixing bowl, and mix again.

Grease a small round or oval casserole dish, and pour in the zucchini mixture. Sprinkle the grated cheese on top.

Bake for 20 minutes until the top of the casserole is slightly brown and it has puffed.

serves 6

❧ Seafood ❧

The bounty of the sea holds a highly esteemed place in New England cuisine. It wasn't always so; the earliest settlers, the Pilgrims, didn't like seafood much and weren't very good at catching it. With the help of the local Indians, they learned quickly, however, and within a very short time they were enjoying and exporting the abundance of the waters around them. And abundant the waters were. Lobsters, shellfish, the ubiquitous cod and many other kinds of seafood were there for the asking. Until into this century, oysters and lobsters were commonplace meals, not the luxuries they are today.

In Colonial times, seafood was usually prepared by baking, sometimes in deep sand pits lined with heated rocks and steaming seaweed, or in large, hearth-cooked stews or "fish-pots" slowly simmered over glowing embers. Both methods are simple—and they preserve the fresh, robust taste of the seafood.

Today's New England cooks are faithful to their Colonial heritage. Fish stews of various sorts are still popular, as is that summer pleasure, the clambake. In this chapter you'll find recipes for the traditional favorites as well as ways to cook seafood that the cooks of bygone days could never have imagined.

❧ Broiled Bluefish with Spicy Sauce

1½ to 2 pounds blue fish fillets
salt to taste
freshly ground black pepper to taste
2 tablespoons melted butter
Spicy Sauce:
6 red pimentos, finely chopped
4 teaspoons tarragon vinegar
6 shallots, finely chopped
4 egg yolks, beaten
¾ cup melted butter
½ teaspoon dried tarragon
½ teaspoon chopped parsley

Season the fillets with salt and pepper.

Preheat the broiler.

Mix the olive oil and butter in a bowl and dip the fillets in the mixture. Place the fillets in a broiling pan and broil for 8 to 10 minutes for the first side and 5 to 8 minutes for the second side.

To make the spicy sauce, combine the pimentos, vinegar, and shallots in a saucepan and cook together until almost all the liquid is gone. Stir in the egg yolks. Transfer the mixture to the top of a double boiler and cook, stirring constantly, over hot water until the mixture thickens. Add the melted butter little by little until the mixture is as thick as mayonnaise. Add the tarragon and parsley. Serve on the side at once with the fish.

serves 4

❧ Steamed Soft-Shell Clams

100 soft-shell clams
1 cup melted butter
1 small onion, sliced
1 tablespoon lemon juice

Scrub the clams thoroughly. Place them in a large pot with 1 cup cold water and the sliced onion. Cover the pot tightly and bring to a boil, stirring once or twice. Do not let the clams come to a frothy boil. After 5 to 8 minutes, all the clams should be opened. Discard any clams that do not open. Remove the clams from the pot and save the broth.

Strain the broth through a piece of cheesecloth and serve with the clams.

Melt the butter and mix in the lemon juice. Serve with the clams for dipping.

serves 5 to 6

Fried Clam Cakes

2 tablespoons butter
½ shallot, finely minced
1¼ cup soft unflavored bread crumbs
2 eggs, beaten
1 pound cooked clams, minced and drained
½ cup chopped celery
1 tablespoon lemon juice
2 tablespoons chopped parsley
½ teaspoon salt
white pepper to taste
½ cup heavy cream
1 egg
peanut or vegetable oil

Melt the butter in a saucepan. Add the shallot and sauté until tender.

Add ½ cup bread crumbs, the clams, celery, lemon juice, parsley, salt and a dusting of white pepper. Cook over medium heat, stirring constantly, for 5 minutes.

Slowly fold the cream into the clam mixture, stirring with a wooden spoon until blended.

Pour the clam mixture into a bowl and chill for two hours.

In a shallow bowl, beat the egg thoroughly with a little water unti it froths.

Spread the remaining bread crumbs on a large plate.

Remove the clam mixture from the refrigerator, and shape into flat, 2-inch round cakes.

Dip each cake in the bread crumbs, covering it completely. Then dip each cake in the beaten egg, and then coat again with another layer of bread crumbs.

After each cake is prepared, set it on spread paper towels to dry. Allow the cakes to dry for at least 10 minutes.

Coat a skillet with a thin layer of peanut or vegetable oil, and fry the cakes, a few at a time, over a moderate heat, until they are crisp and golden brown.

serves 6

Fried Clams

1 egg, separated
½ cup milk
1 tablespoon butter
salt to taste
½ cup flour
24 little neck or 18 cherrystone clams, shelled
vegetable oil

Beat the yolk into half the milk in a mixing bowl.

Stir in the butter, salt and flour and beat until smooth. Then beat in the remaining milk, a little at a time.

Beat the egg white until it is stiff enough to peak. Fold it into the batter and mix until thoroughly blended.

Pour a thin layer of vegetable oil into a skillet over moderate heat.

Dip each clam in the batter and fry, a few clams at a time. Replenish the oil as needed. Clams are done when golden brown and tender.

serves 4

✂ Clam Omelet

6 eggs, separated
6 tablespoons butter
1 cup milk
½ teaspoon salt
¼ teaspoon freshly ground black pepper
1 cup chopped clams
2 tablespoons melted butter

Melt the 6 tablespoons butter in an omelet pan over low heat.

Manwhile, beat the egg yolks in a bowl until blended. Add the milk, stir well, and add the salt, pepper, and clams. Stir and add the 2 tablespoons melted butter.

In a separate bowl, beat the egg whites until stiff but not dry. Fold them into the egg yolk mixture.

Pour the egg mixture into the omelet pan (the butter should all be melted by now). With a spatula, lift the omelet as it sets so that the butter reaches every part. When the omelet is golden brown, fold it and serve very hot.

serves 4

✂ Summer Clambake

18 lobsters (or 1 for each person), at least 1
    pound each
36 ears of corn, with the husks and silk removed
    (save the husks)
18 baking potatoes in their skins, scrubbed
6 whole frying chickens, quartered
9 quarts steamer clams
4 pounds butter
salt and pepper shakers

Here's a feast that's perfect for an ocean or lakefront beach party! You'll need some special equipment before you start: a steel trash can with lid, enough wood for a large fire that will burn for an hour, a sand-dug fire pit, 18 large pieces of cheesecloth at least a yard square, a ball of twine, and a strong standing iron grill.

First, build a large hot fire in the pit. Then get at least two people to help you prepare the food.

Lay about ½ quart of the clams in the center of each cheesecloth square. Next build layers of lobster, corn, potatoes, and chicken on top of the clams, putting a thin layer of corn husks between each layer of food. When all the food has been piled in mounds on the cloth, draw in the corners of the cheesecloth and tie them tightly with twine so that they form closed sacks.

Take the remaining corn husks (or seaweed if you're near the ocean) and put them in a thick layer in the bottom of the trash can. Add enough sea water or clear lake water to cover the layer of husks or seaweed.

Lay the food sacks in the trash can on top of the husks or seaweed and cover the can. Place the iron grill over the center of the fire, and carefully put the can on the grill. Place a heavy rock on the lid to secure it tightly.

Keep the fire hot and roaring for 1 hour while the food bakes. Check every 20 minutes or so to see if the food is becoming scorched. If it is, then the water is evaporating too quickly. Add small amounts of water to keep the can full of steam.

If the fire gets too high or a bit out of hand, douse it with water a little around the edges.

After the food has baked for a full hour, put out plenty of butter, salt and pepper and serve everyone with as much as they can eat.

serves 18 to 20

✻ Codfish Pie

¾ pound fresh codfish, cubed
¼ pound thickly sliced salt pork or bacon
1 onion, finely chopped
3 tablespoons flour
freshly ground black pepper to taste
2½ cups milk
1 cup diced cooked potatoes
1½ cups flour
2 teaspoons baking powder
¼ teaspoon salt
6 tablespoons melted shortening
light cream

Put the codfish in a large kettle and add enough cold water to cover. Bring the water quickly to a boil, then reduce the heat, cover and simmer for about 15 minutes, until the fish is tender and easily flaked.

Drain the codfish well and flake it with a fork. Set aside.

Put the salt pork or bacon in a skillet and cook over medium heat until the pieces are brown and crisp. Remove the pieces from the skillet and save. Spoon off and discard half the drippings. Add the onion to the skillet and sauté until tender. Then sprinkle in the 3 tablespoons of flour, stirring constantly with a wooden spoon, until all the flour is evenly blended. While continuing to stir, add the pepper and gradually blend in the milk. Cook until the mixture begins to thicken. Stir in the codfish, pork or bacon pieces and potatoes and cook for about 2 minutes, or until all the ingredients are thoroughly blended. Turn off the heat and let the skillet cool.

In a mixing bowl, combine the flour, baking powder and salt. Stir in the shortening and enough light cream to make the dough soft and workable.

Knead the dough for about a minute, then roll it out into a ¼-inch crust.

Preheat the oven to 400°.

Pour the codfish mixture into a deep, butter-greased baking dish. Lay the crust over the top of the baking dish, trim and seal the edges.

Bake the pie for about 25 minutes, or until the crust is golden brown and flaky.

serves 4

✻ Cod Broiled in Lemon Butter

2 pounds codfish fillets
6 tablespoons melted butter
3 tablespoons lemon juice
1 teaspoon salt
½ teaspoon freshly ground black pepper
2 tablespoons soft, fresh unflavored bread
    crumbs

Preheat the broiler to its highest temperature.

In a baking dish mix the melted butter, lemon juice, salt, and pepper. Dip the cod fillets in the mixture until they are coated on both sides. Arrange the fillets in one layer in the dish.

Broil the fish 3 to 4 inches from the flame for 5 minutes. Baste the fillets with the pan liquids. Sprinkle the bread crumbs over the fillets and broil for 5 minutes longer or until the fish flakes easily.

Serve the fillets at once with some of the pan liquids poured over them.

The fortune of one of the great New England families, the Cabots, was based on the humble cod. George Cabot was captain of a codfish schooner when he was just 18, in 1770.

serves 4

❧ Fried Soft-Shell Crabs

12 soft-shell crabs
2 eggs, beaten
½ cup flour
½ teaspoon salt
¼ teaspoon freshly ground black pepper
½ cup butter

Wash the crabs in cold water and dry thoroughly.

In a small bowl, beat the eggs. In another bowl, combine the flour, salt, and pepper. Dip the crabs in the eggs and then dredge them in the flour mixture. Shake off the excess flour.

Heat the butter in a skillet over a low flame. Place in the skillet as many crabs as will lie flat at one time. Fry the crabs until they are browned and crisp on the edges. Turn and fry until the other side is browned. Serve very hot with butter.

serves 6

❧ Broiled Soft-Shell Crabs

12 soft-shell crabs
½ pound butter
9 tablespoons lemon juice
⅛ teaspoon cayenne pepper
salt to taste
freshly ground black pepper to taste
½ cup flour
Sauce:
1½ tablespoons butter
1 teaspoon flour
1 cup fish stock or watersalt to taste
freshly ground black pepper to taste
2 egg yolks, beaten
¼ cup cream
1 tablespoon lemon juice

Wash the crabs in cold water and dry well.

In a small saucepan melt the butter. Add the lemon juice and cayenne.

Preheat the broiler.

Sprinkle the crabs with salt and pepper. Dip them in the butter sauce and then dredge them in the flour, shaking off the excess.

Lay the crabs on a broiler rack and place them 4 inches from the heat for 8 minutes, turning frequently.

To make the sauce, melt the butter in the top of a double boiler over hot but not boiling water. Blend in the flour; stir in the fish stock or water. Simmer for 10 minutes and season with salt and pepper. Remove the saucepan from the heat. Add the egg yolks and the cream. Return to heat and cook, stirring constantly, for 3 minutes. Add the lemon juice and serve immediately, poured over the crabs.

serves 6

❧ Boiled Lobster

4 1- to 2-pound live lobsters
4 quarts boiling water
6 whole peppercorns
¼ pound melted butter

Place the water in a large pot with the salt and peppercorns. Bring to a boil.

Wash the lobsters under cold running water. When the water is boiling rapidly, plunge the lobsters head-first into the water. Cover tightly and bring the water back to a boil. Reduce heat and simmer 15 minutes for 1-pound lobsters or 20 minutes for 2-pound lobsters.

Remove the lobsters from the water and place them in the sink until they are cool enough to handle. Serve whole with melted butter for dipping.

To eat a boiled lobster, first pull off the claws. Use a nutcracker to break the claws. Pull out the meat. Turn the body of the lobster soft-side up and bend it backward until the tail breaks off from the body. Break off the tail flippers. Pick up the tail and push the meat out in one large piece from the flipper end. The body of the lobster contains the edible tomalley, or liver, and the delicious roe or coral if the lobster is female. Eating a lobster is never a neat operation. Bibs, napkins, fingerbowls and towels are suggested.

serves 4

✄ Broiled Lobster

4 1- to 2-pound live lobsters
⅛ cup melted butter
paprika
bread crumbs
Basting sauce:
½ pound butter
1 clove garlic, crushed
½ teaspoon parsley, chopped

Split the lobsters from head to tail with a sharp, heavy knife. Remove the entrails and roe. Crack the claw shells with a nutcracker. Place the lobsters on their backs in a broiling pan. Brush them with the melted butter. Be sure to brush the claws as well to keep them from drying out. Sprinkle paprika and bread crumbs over the exposed meat.

Preheat the broiler to high.

Place the pan under the broiler for about 10 minutes, being careful to avoid under- or overbroiling. Turn the lobsters over and broil for about 8 minutes. As the lobsters broil, baste them frequently with the sauce.

To make the basting sauce, melt the butter in a small saucepan. Stir in the garlic and parsley.

serves 4

✄ Oyster-Stuffed Lobsters

2 medium onions, chopped
1 celery stalk with leaves, chopped
4 tablespoons butter
4 white mushrooms, sliced
2 cups shelled oysters, with liquid
4 cups bread crumbs
2 tablespoons chopped parsley
1 teaspoon salt
freshly ground black pepper to taste
½ teaspoon dried thyme
4 lobsters, 1 pound each or larger

Melt the butter in a shallow skillet. Add the onion and celery and sauté until they are tender. Add the mushrooms and cook 2 to 3 minutes until they are a glazed, golden brown.

Strain the oysters and save their liquid. Chop the oysters finely and add them to the skillet. Sauté while stirring until the pieces begin to curl and become tender.

Add the bread crumbs, parlsey, salt, pepper and thyme. Stir all ingredients together with a wooden spoon. While stirring, slowly add the reserved oyster liquid until the stuffing is moist and clings together.

With a large, heavy knife, split the lobsters and remove the entrails and roe. Crack the claw shells with a nutcracker.

Place the lobsters split-side up on a foil-covered broiling rack. Stuff the cavities with the oyster stuffing. Fold the foil over the lobsters and broil for about 15 minutes. Unfold the foil and broil again for 3 to 5 minutes.

Serve with melted butter and lemon wedges.

serves 4

❧ Cider Flounder

6 flounder fillets
salt to taste
freshly ground black pepper to taste
3 tablespoons chopped shallots
2 to 3 cups apple cider
3 tablespoons butter
2 tablespoons flour
1 teaspoon chopped parsley

Preheat the oven to 375°.

Wash and dry the flounder fillets. Sprinkle them with salt and pepper.

Place the fillets in a buttered baking dish and sprinkle with shallots. Add just enough cider to cover and bake for 20 minutes. Remove flounder to a hot serving platter.

Pour the liquid in the baking pan into a saucepan. Add the butter and heat until the butter melts. Blend in the flour. Stir until the sauce begins to thicken, then cook 5 minutes longer, stirring occasionally. Add the parsley and pour the sauce over the fish.

serves 6

❧ Crab-Stuffed Haddock

1 3-pound haddock, cleaned
1½ cups flaked crab meat
¼ cup finely chopped celery
½ cup finely chopped tart apple
1 tablespoon chopped green pepper
1 cup unflavored bread crumbs
salt to taste
freshly ground black pepper to taste
2 tablespoons melted butter
1 lime, sliced

Preheat the oven to 400°.

Wipe the fish clean and dry gently.

In a mixing bowl, combine the crab meat, celery, apple, green pepper, bread crumbs, egg and salt and pepper to taste. Stuff the haddock with the mixture. Close the cavity with thread or skewers.

Place the fish in a buttered baking dish. Drizzle the melted butter over the fish. Bake 35 minutes. Serve garnished with the lime slices.

serves 4

❧ Baked Halibut

3 pounds halibut fillets
12 tablespoons butter
4 tablespoons lemon juice
1 teaspoon salt
½ teaspoon freshly ground black pepper
6 scallions, chopped (including green parts)
5 tablespoons chopped parsley

Preheat the oven to 350°. Wash and gently dry the fillets.

Melt the butter in a saucepan over low heat. Stir in the lemon juice, salt, pepper, scallions, and parsley. Pour half this sauce into a shallow baking dish. Place the fillets in the dish and pour the remaining sauce on top. Bake 15 to 20 minutes, or until the fish flakes easily.

serves 4

❧ Broiled Salmon Steaks with Lemon Butter

4 salmon steaks
1 teaspoon salt
½ teaspoon black pepper
¼ cup melted butter
¼ teaspoon grated lemon rind
¼ cup lemon juice
1 lemon, sliced

Preheat the broiler.

Sprinkle the salmon steaks on both sides with the salt and pepper. Place the steaks in a broiling pan lined with aluminum foil.

In a small bowl, mix together the melted butter, lemon rind and lemon juice. Brush the fish lightly with the mixture.

Broil the fish 2 inches from the heat for 5 to 6 minutes or until slightly browned. Brush the fish again with the lemon mixture, turn carefully, and brush the other side. Broil 5 to 6 minutes longer or until the fish flakes easily. Brush with the remaining lemon mixture and serve garnished with lemon slices.

serves 4

❊ Fried Mussels

48 medium-sized mussels
2 eggs, beaten
½ cup unflavored breadcrumbs
1 cup olive oil
watercress
lemon slices

Scrub, rinse, and debeard the mussels.

Steam the mussels for 5 to 8 minutes in a large pot until they open. Discard any mussels that do not open. Shell the mussels and reserve some of their liquid. Chill.

Dry the mussels thoroughly on paper towels. In a small bowl beat the eggs with 2 tablespoons of the cold mussel liquid. Dip the mussels in the egg mixture and roll in the breadcrumbs.

In a deep skillet heat the olive oil to 375°. Fry the mussels until golden brown. Drain on paper towels. Serve hot, garnished with watercress and lemon slices.

serves 4

❊ Scalloped Oysters

1 quart shelled oysters, with liquid
1 cup corn flake crumbs
1 cup unflavored bread crumbs
½ teaspoon salt
¼ teaspoon freshly ground black pepper
2 tablespoons sherry
2 tablespoons light cream
½ cup melted butter
1 garlic clove, crushed

Preheat the oven to 400°.

In a mixing bowl combine the corn flake crumbs and the bread crumbs. Add the salt and pepper. Stir in the sherry, cream, butter, and garlic.

Butter a shallow baking dish and place a layer of the crumb mixture on the bottom. Place a layer of oysters over this. Continue to fill the dish with alternate layers of the crumb mixture and the oysters. Be sure not to have more than two layers of oysters. Pour the oyster liquid over the top. Top with crumbs and dot with butter. Bake for 30 minutes.

serves 6

❊ Oyster Fry

36 to 48 oysters, shelled
1 cup fine unflavored bread crumbs
½ teaspoon salt
¼ teaspoon freshly ground black pepper
2 eggs
½ teaspoon Tabasco sauce
1 cup olive oil

Dry the oysters thoroughly on paper towels.

Combine the bread crumbs with the salt and pepper. Dip the oysters in the mixture.

In a small bowl beat the eggs and Tabasco sauce together. Dip the oysters in this mixture, then roll them in the crumbs again.

In a deep skillet, heat the olive oil to 375°. Fry the oysters until they are golden brown. Drain on paper towels.

serves 4

✳ Scrambled Oysters

36 oysters, shelled and drained
salt to taste
freshly ground black pepper to taste
7 eggs, beaten
4 tablespoons light cream
½ cup unseasoned croutons
1 tablespoon butter
parsley sprigs

Chop the oysters. Season them with salt and pepper.

Beat the eggs in a mixing bowl. Stir in the cream and add the croutons. Mix until the croutons are coated with the egg mixture.

Melt the butter in a skillet over moderate heat. Add the egg mixture. When the eggs begin to get firm, stir in the oysters and scramble. Serve garnished with parsley.

serves 4 to 6

✳ Fried Scallops

1 pint whole bay scallops
2 tablespoons flour
1 egg
¼ cup milk
½ cup unflavored bread crumbs
¼ cup flour
1 cup vegetable oil

Place the scallops on paper towels to dry. Dredge the scallops in the 2 tablespoons flour.

In a small bowl, beat the egg and milk together. Dip the floured scallops into the mixture.

In another bowl, combine ¼ cup flour and the bread crumbs. Roll the scallops in the mixture.

Heat the vegetable oil to 375° in a deep skillet. Drop the scallops, a few at a time, into the oil. Fry until browned, about 4 minutes. Skim the oil and reheat as necessary.

Drain scallops on paper towels. Serve very hot.

serves 4

✳ Scallop Stew

2 pounds scallops
½ cup dry vermouth or white wine
1 garlic clove, chopped
5 tablespoons olive oil
2 cups thinly sliced Spanish red onions
2 cups plum tomatoes, peeled and chopped
3 tablespoons butter
salt to taste
freshly ground black pepper to taste
2 tablespoons chopped parsley

Place the scallops with their liquid in a small bowl. Add the vermouth and garlic and let stand for 30 minutes.

In a large skillet heat the olive oil. Sauté the onions until they are translucent and lightly golden. Add the tomatoes, cover, and cook over moderate heat until the tomatoes soften.

Add the butter and scallops with the marinade. Season with salt and pepper to taste. Simmer, uncovered, until the scallops are opaque. Sprinkle with parsley and simmer 1 minute more. Serve hot.

serves 4

✂ Batter Shrimp

1 pound shrimp, cleaned, shelled and deveined
1½ tablespoons olive oil
¼ teaspoon salt
¼ teaspoon freshly ground black pepper
2 tablespoons lemon juice
vegetable oil for frying
Batter:
1 cup flour
¼ teaspoon salt
1 egg, beaten
1½ tablespoons olive oil
¾ cup warm water

In a small bowl beat together the olive oil with the salt, pepper, and lemon juice. Place the shrimp in a bowl and pour this mixture over. Let stand for 30 minutes.

To make the batter, mix the flour and salt in a bowl. In a separate bowl, combine the beaten egg, olive oil, and water. Add this gradually to the flour, beating until smooth.

Thread the shrimp onto small skewers or long toothpicks and dip them into the batter. In a deep skillet, heat to 375°: enough vegetable oil to fill the skillet to a depth of ¼ inch. Fry the shrimp until they are golden brown. Drain on paper towels.

serves 4

✂ Shrimp and Corn Soufflé

6 ears fresh corn
3 eggs, separated
2 tablespoons sugar
1 tablespoon melted butter
½ teaspoon salt
1½ pounds shrimp, cooked, peeled, and deveined.

Preheat the oven to 300°.

Cut the corn from the cob.

Beat the egg yolks in a mixing bowl until blended. Stir in the corn, sugar, melted butter, salt, and shrimp.

In a separate bowl beat the egg whites until stiff but not dry. Fold them into the yolk mixture.

Turn the egg mixture into a buttered 1½-quart soufflé dish, cover, and set the dish in a pan of hot water. Bake for 1 hour or until firm. Remove the cover for the last 15 minutes to let the top of the soufflé brown. Serve *immediately.*

serves 4 to 6

✂ Stuffed Sea Trout

1 5- to 6-pound sea trout, cleaned
¼ cup diced salt pork
1 shallot, finely chopped
1 pound fresh shrimp, shelled, deveined, and chopped
½ cup sliced white mushrooms
¾ cup unflavored bread crumbs
1 tablespoon chopped parsley
¼ teaspoon dried thyme
salt to taste
freshly ground black pepper to taste
¼ cup lemon juice

Wipe the fish clean and dry gently. Rub the fish cavity with some salt.

Heat a skillet and add the salt pork. Cook until the pieces are crisp. Remove the pork and reserve.

Add the shallot to the drippings and sauté over medium heat until tender. Add the mushrooms and shrimp to the skillet, increase the heat and cook quickly, stirring frequently, for 5 minutes, or until the shrimp are pink and firm.

Add the mushrooms, bread crumbs, parsley, thyme, salt, pepper and pork pieces. Stir all the ingredients together.

Preheat the oven to 400°.

Stuff the cavity of the sea trout with the mixture. Pour half the lemon juice over the stuffing.

Place the fish on a buttered baking dish. Close the cavity, using thread or skewers. Brush some melted butter over the skin and dust with salt and pepper. Sprinkle the remaining lemon juice over the fish.

Bake for 40 minutes or until the fish meat is white, firm to the touch, and flakes easily.

serves 6

✖ Butter-Stuffed Trout

1 4-pound trout or 2 2-pound trouts
2 tablespoons dry sherry
¾ cup butter
1 scallion, minced
2 tablespoons minced parsley
½ cup finely chopped mushrooms
1 garlic clove, crushed
1 teaspoon salt
black pepper to taste
1 cup dry white wine
1 cup heavy cream
2 egg yolks
¼ cup brandy, heated

Clean and rinse the fish. Pat dry. Brush the inside of the fish with sherry. Chill for 2 hours.

Preheat the oven to 375°.

In a small bowl cream the butter and scallion together. Add the parsley, mushrooms, garlic and salt. Mix until well combined.

Place the fish in a baking pan. Spread the inside of the fish with three-quarters of the butter mixture. Spread the remaining mixture on the outside of the fish. Pour the wine over the fish and bake for 45 minutes. Baste frequently.

Remove the fish from the oven and carefully transfer it to a heat-proof serving dish.

Strain the liquid in the baking pan into a saucepan. Simmer the liquid until it is reduced by half.

In a small bowl combine the cream and egg yolks. Slowly beat the hot liquid into the egg mixture. Cook over low heat for 2 to 3 minutes. Stir constantly. Season with salt and pepper to taste.

Pour the heated brandy over the fish. Carefully light the brandy and baste the fish with the spirit until the flame dies out.

Pour the cream sauce over the fish and serve immediately.

serves 4

✖ Pan-Fried Trout

4 ½-pound trouts
2 teaspoons salt
¼ teaspoon black pepper
½ cup yellow corn meal
½ cup flour
3 tablespoons butter
6 tablespoons vegetable oil
1 lemon, quartered

Clean and wash the trout, but leave the heads and tails intact. Pat dry. Rub the fish inside and out with the salt and pepper.

In a large bowl combine the flour and corn meal. Roll the trout, one at a time, in the mixture until well coated. Shake off excess.

Heat the butter and oil together in a large skillet. When very hot, add the coated trout. Fry the fish unti golden brown, about 4 to 5 minutes per side.

Carefully remove the fish from the skillet and drain briefly on paper towels. Serve hot with lemon wedges.

serves 4

❧ Stuffed Striped Bass with Raisin Sauce

1 4- to 5-pound striped bass, cleaned
2 cups unflavored bread crumbs
hot water
2 tablespoons butter
1 tablespoon chopped onion
1 tablespoon chopped parsley
1 tablespoon drained capers
1 teaspoon salt
½ teaspoon freshly ground black pepper
1 egg, beaten
Raisin Sauce:
2 tablespoons butter
2 tablespoons flour
1 teaspoon salt
¼ teaspoon freshly ground black pepper
1 tablespoon brown sugar
1½ cups water
¼ cup chopped raisins
¼ cup ground almonds
2 tablespoons drained grated horseradish
¼ cup fine unflavored bread crumbs
¼ cup lemon juice

Preheat the oven to 400°. Wipe the fish clean and dry gently.

In a mixing bowl moisten the bread crumbs with hot water. Remove the crumbs from the bowl and press them dry in a clean kitchen towel. Return the crumbs to the bowl and add the butter, onion, parsley, capers, salt, pepper and egg. Stuff the fish with this mixture and sew the cavity closed or close it with skewers. Put the fish into a buttered baking dish and bake for 40 to 50 minutes, or 10 minutes per pound.

To make the raisin sauce, melt the butter in a saucepan and blend in the flour, salt, pepper, brown sugar, and water. Stir the mixture until it begins to boil, then add the raisins, ground almonds, and horseradish. Heat thoroughly. Just before serving, add the bread crumbs and lemon juice. Pour the sauce over the fish and serve.

serves 4 to 6

❧ Cranberry-Stuffed Mackerel

2 mackerel, totaling 3 pounds
½ pound cranberries
4 tablespoons unflavored breadcrumbs
4 tablespoons butter
1 teaspoon anchovy paste
salt to taste
black pepper to taste
⅛ teaspoon cayenne pepper

Preheat the oven to 350°.

Split the mackerel down the spine and remove the bones.

Chop the cranberries coarsely. In a mixing bowl, combine the cranberries, breadcrumbs, butter, anchovy paste, salt, pepper and cayenne pepper.

Stuff each mackerel with the cranberry mixture. Wrap the fish in aluminum foil and place them in a buttered baking dish. Bake for 30 minutes. Carefully remove the foil and serve.

If gooseberries are available, substitute them for the cranberries.

serves 4

❧ Broiled Weakfish

6 weakfish fillets
2 tablespoons tarragon vinegar
2 tablespoons olive oil
¼ teaspoon freshly ground black pepper
½ teaspoon salt
1 lemon, quartered
Drawn butter sauce:
3 tablespoons flour
3 tablespoons melted butter
¼ teaspoon salt
¼ teaspoon freshly ground black pepper
1½ cups hot water
3 tablespoons butter, cut into small pieces
1 teaspoon lemon juice

Wash and dry the fillets. Rub them with the vinegar.

Preheat the broiler to medium.

In a small bowl combine the oil, salt, and pepper. Roll the fillets in the oil mixture.

Place the fillets in a greased broiler pan and broil slowly, basting frequently with the olive oil mixture and turning once.

To make the drawn butter sauce, combine the flour, melted butter, salt, and pepper in a medium saucepan. Slowly stir in the hot water and boil for 5 minutes.

Lower the heat and add the pieces of cut-up butter alternately with the lemon juice. Stir well and serve hot over fish. Garnish with lemon quarters.

Weakfish is another name for sea trout.

serves 4 to 6

Colonial Fish Pot

1 tablespoon salt
1 tablespoon paprika
½ teaspoon white pepper
½ teaspoon dried thyme
¼ cup flour
1 pound thickly cut cod fillet
1 pound thickly cut haddock steak
1 pound flounder fillet
6 bacon strips, diced
4 onions, sliced
6 tablespoons butter
12 white mushroom caps
2 leeks, sliced crosswise
¼ pound Edam or Gouda cheese, diced
3 cups milk
6 eggs, beaten
salt to taste

Mix the salt, paprika, pepper, thyme and flour together on a plate.

Dredge the cod, haddock and flounder in the flour mixture, coating all sides. Cut the fish into large chunks.

Cook the bacon in a large heavy pot until half done. Add the fish chunks and the onions to the drippings and sauté, stirring often with a wooden spoon, until the onions are tender and browned.

Preheat the oven to 325°.

Use half the butter to grease a large casserole dish. Pour in the fish, bacon and onions, and add the mushrooms and leeks.

Mix the diced cheese, milk and beaten eggs in a bowl and pour over the fish in the casserole.

Bake for 40 minutes. Remove the dish from the oven and dot the casserole with remaining butter. Bake again for 5 minutes.

serves 4

Seafood Stew

3 garlic cloves, finely chopped
3 small onions, chopped
vegetable oil
½ teaspoon dried thyme
¼ cup chopped parsley
¼ teaspoon caraway seeds
1 bay leaf
2 cups white wine
14 ounces whole, peeled plum tomatoes
¾ pound small squid
1½ pounds cod fillets
1 pound flounder fillets
1 pound striped bass fillets
¼ teaspoon salt
freshly ground black pepper to taste
14 soft-shell clams, scrubbed and rinsed

Pour a thin layer of vegetable oil into a Dutch oven or deep stew pot over moderate heat. Add the garlic and onion and sauté until transparent but not browned. Add the thyme, parsley, caraway seeds, bay leaf and white wine. Raise the heat and bring the ingredients to a boil. Cover the pot, reduce the heat, and simmer for about 10 minutes.

Add the tomatoes and lay the squid on top. Simmer, covered, for 10 more minutes.

Lay the cod, flounder and bass fillets over the squid, one at a time, and dust with the salt and pepper. Cover and let simmer for 12 minutes.

Spread the clams around the edges of the pot, cover, and simmer for 10 to 15 minutes, or until the clams open and are tender and opaque.

serves 6

Tile Fish Simmered in Wine

3 pounds tile fish steaks
1 cup white wine or dry vermouth
salt to taste
black pepper to taste
4 tablespoons butter
2 tablespoons olive oil
2 tablespoons Dijon-style mustard
2 tablespoons lemon juice
4 tablespoons light cream

Sprinkle the steaks with salt and pepper on both sides.

Melt the butter in a large skillet and blend in the olive oil. Add the steaks and lightly brown on both sides. Add the wine and simmer, covered, for 5 to 8 minutes.

To make the sauce, mix together in a saucepan the mustard, lemon juice and cream. Heat thoroughly and pour over fish.

serves 4

Baked Bluefish

1 4- to 5-pound bluefish
salt to taste
black pepper to taste
4 tablespoons mayonnaise
2 lemons, sliced
4 scallions, chopped (including green part)

Preheat the oven to 400°.

Rub the fish with salt and pepper inside and out. Coat the fish with the mayonnaise inside and out.

Place the fish in a baking dish lined with aluminum foil. Arrange the lemon slices on top of the fish and sprinkle the fish with the chopped scallions.

Bake the fish for 40 to 50 minutes, or 10 minutes per pound.

serves 4 to 6

Baked Swordfish Steaks

2 pounds swordfish steaks
3 tablespoons olive oil
1/4 teaspoon paprika
1/2 teaspoon salt
1/2 cup corn meal
4 teaspoons flour

Preheat the oven to 350°

Pour the olive oil into a shallow baking dish and blend in the paprika and salt.

Place the swordfish steaks in the dish one at a time and turn to coat both sides with the oil mixture. Sprinkle the steaks with the corn meal and flour.

Return the steaks to the baking dish and bake for 5 minutes. Remove the dish from the oven and place it under the broiler until the coating is golden brown, about 15 to 20 minutes. Do not turn fish as it broils.

serves 4 to 6

Cider Flounder

Cod Broiled in Lemon Butter

Stuffed Acorn Squash

Boston Brown Bread

Red Flannel Hash

Pork Chops with Cranberries

Maple Barbecue

Toll House Cookies

❧ Poultry and Meat ❧

Famous as New England is for seafood dishes, meat and poultry also have an important place. In fact, during the early years of Colonial settlement, meat and game were the mainstays of the New England diet. Seafood only became popular after the colonists had learned to "hunt the sea" like the Indians.

The accent in these dishes is on simplicity. For the most part, traditional New Englanders prefer thick, hearty stews, flavorful hams, chops, roasts and other full dinners for hungry, hard-working families.

Classic New England meals such as Boiled Dinner, Red Flannel Hash or Chicken with Crab Stuffing are excellent family meals. For special holidays, something traditional but also unusual is called for. Try Roast Goose with Fancy Fruit Stuffing, Roast Stuffed Squab or Baked Venison for a different taste.

At the first Thanksgiving in 1621, the Pilgrims feasted on wild turkey. We don't know with what, if anything, they stuffed the bird, but the traditional New England approach has always been sausage and sage. Of course, the recipe is in this chapter.

❧ Chicken with Crab Meat Stuffing

2 medium-sized chickens (1½ to 2 pounds), split in half
6 tablespoons butter
2 tablespoons soy sauce
¼ teaspoon freshly ground black pepper
¼ teaspoon ground ginger
2 teaspoons paprika
½ pound mushrooms, sliced
½ cup sherry
1 tablespoon chopped parsley
Stuffing:
3 cups cubed stale white bread
¼ cup light cream
¾ pound uncooked crab meat
¼ cup melted butter
¼ teaspoon white pepper
1 teaspoon salt
1 teaspoon Dijon-style mustard
½ teaspoon dried thyme
¼ teaspoon dried rosemary
¼ teaspoon dried sage

Preheat the oven to 350°

In a mixing bowl, knead 2 tablespoons of the butter with the fingers until the butter is soft. Add the soy sauce, pepper and ginger and mix together into a paste.

Rub the chicken halves with the seasoned butter, working it well into the skin, and put extra amounts of butter on and under the wings. Place the chicken parts, skin-side up, in a large baking dish and bake for 30 minutes.

Melt the remaining butter in a saucepan, and add the mushrooms, sherry and parsley. Sauté over medium heat, stirring constantly, until the mushrooms are tender. Cover the saucepan and remove it from the heat.

While the chicken is baking, prepare the stuffing by mixing all the ingredients in a large bowl and working them together with the hands. Add more water if the stuffing is not moist enough.

Turn the partially cooked chicken halves over. Press the stuffing into the cavity with a wooden spoon.

Turn the halves skin-side up again in the baking dish. Spoon the butter and mixture from the saucepan over each of the halves.

Bake for 35 minutes longer, or until the chicken is firm and tender, basting often.

serves 4

✼ Chicken Skillet Stew

4 tablespoons vegetable or peanut oil
1½ pounds boned chicken breast, cut into 2-inch pieces
4 medium-sized zucchini, sliced
2 medium-sized onions, chopped
2 garlic cloves, minced
1 bay leaf
1 celery stalk with leaves, chopped
1 carrot, chopped
2 large new or red potatoes, quartered
1½ cups chicken broth
1 teaspoon salt
¼ teaspoon freshly ground black pepper
2 cups sliced mushrooms
1 tablespoon cider vinegar
1 tablespoon chopped dill
2 tablespoons chopped parsley

Heat the oil in a large skillet. Add the chicken pieces and sauté them quickly until they are white and firm.

Add half the zucchini, and all of the onion, garlic, bay leaf, celery, carrot and potatoes to the skillet. Sauté, stirring constantly, for 5 minutes. Add 1 cup of the chicken broth and the salt and pepper and let simmer for 15 minutes.

With a slotted spoon, move the potatoes and chicken to one side of the skillet. Mash the vegetables into a coarse liquid with the spoon.

Stir all the ingredients together again, and add the remaining zucchini, the mushrooms, vinegar, dill, 1 tablespoon of the parsley and the remaining chicken broth.

Let the stew simmer for another 5 to 10 minutes, stirring often, until the zucchini are tender but still bright green.

Serve in a heated ceramic bowl. Sprinkle the remaining parsley over the top.

serves 4

✼ Golden Chicken Fricassee

2 whole frying chickens with giblets, cut into serving pieces
2 cups chicken broth
2 cups water
¼ teaspoon ground mace
1½ teaspoons salt
1 teaspoon saffron threads
¾ cup butter
1 pound white mushrooms, sliced
½ cup flour
freshly ground black pepper to taste
½ cup dry white wine
parsley sprigs
lemon slices

Prepare the giblet stock at least 4 hours before you are ready to serve the meal. Put the necks, wing tips, backbones and giblets (except livers) of the chickens into a sauce-pan. Add the broth and water, cover and bring quickly to a boil. Reduce the heat and let simmer for about 2 hours, skimming the fat off the surface frequently. Then strain the broth, reserving the giblets, and set it aside to cool.

While the stock simmers rinse the chicken parts and pat them dry. Combine the mace and salt in a small bowl with a little warm water, just enough to make a paste. Rub the parts thoroughly with the paste. Set the parts aside.

An hour before serving, melt the butter in a large Dutch oven or casserole dish. Add the chicken pieces and cook, turning often, for 30 minutes, or until all sides of the pieces are golden brown. Pour off and reserve the butter and drippings from the Dutch oven or dish. Add enough water to the Dutch oven or dish to cover the chicken. Cover and bring the water to a boil. Reduce the heat and simmer for 20 minutes.

Slice the reserved giblets.

Pour enough of the reserved butter/drippings into a saucepan to cover the bottom. Add the mushrooms and sliced giblets and sauté for about 5 minutes, or until the mushrooms begin to give up their liquid. Remove the mushrooms and giblets from the saucepan and set them aside.

Pour the remainder of the reserved butter/drippings into the saucepan over low heat, and slowly add the flour, stirring constantly to avoid lumps. When all of the flour has been blended with the butter, add the giblet stock to the saucepan. Simmer the sauce slowly. Stir in the saffron, making sure it dissolves in the sauce. Add the mushrooms and giblets and season to taste with salt and pepper.

While stirring the sauce, add the white wine. If the sauce is too thick at this point, add some of the broth the chicken parts have been cooking in to thin it.

Place the chicken parts on an oven-proof serving dish, pour the sauce over them and warm in the oven for 5 minutes.

Garnish with parsley sprigs and lemon slices before serving.

serves 6

✂ Chicken Pot Pie

1 4-pound chicken, cut into serving pieces
1 celery stalk
1 carrot
1 onion
1 tablespoon salt
Dough ingredients:
2 cups flour
½ tablespoon salt
2 eggs
2 to 3 tablespoons water
4 medium-sized potatoes, peeled and sliced
6 parsley sprigs, chopped

In a large pot place the chicken pieces, celery, carrot, onion, salt and enough cold water to cover. Bring the mixture to a boil. Reduce the heat, cover the pot tightly, and simmer for 40 minutes, or until the chicken is almost tender when tested with a fork. Turn of the heat. Remove the vegetables and discard them. Leave the chicken in the pot with its broth while you make the dough.

Blend the flour and salt together into a bowl. In the center of this make a small well and drop the eggs in, one at a time. Combine the ingredients thoroughly with the fingers to make a stiff dough. Add the 2 to 3 tablespoons water as needed.

Roll the dough out very thinly on a lightly floured board and cut it into 1-inch square pieces with a pastry wheel or sharp knife.

Bring the chicken and broth back to a boil. Drop the potato slices and pastry squares into the boiling broth, cover, and cook over moderate heat for 20 minutes. Sprinkle in the chopped parsley and serve.

serves 4 to 6

❧ Roast Turkey with Sausage and Sage Dressing

1 14-pound turkey
1½ large loaves stale unsliced wheat bread, cubed
milk
2 large onions, finely chopped
3 celery stalks, finely chopped
4 tablespoons butter
1¾ pounds fresh country sausage
1 teaspoon salt
1 teaspoon freshly ground black pepper
3 teaspoons dried thyme
6 large parsley sprigs, chopped
3 teaspoons dried sage
18 pitted black olives, chopped

To make the dressing, place the bread cubes in a large mixing bowl and soak them in enough milk to moisten them. In a medium-sized skillet sauté the onions and celery together in the butter until they are soft but not brown. Add the vegetables to the bowl with the bread cubes.

In the same skillet, slightly brown the sausages, then break them into pieces with a fork. Add the pieces to the bread-mixture. Add the salt, pepper, thyme, parsley, sage, and olives. Blend well. Stuff the cavity of the turkey with the mixture. Sew the cavity closed or close it with skewers and truss the bird.

Immediately after stuffing, place the bird in a large roasting pan and cover it with several layers of cheesecloth soaked in butter. Bake the bird in a 325° oven for 5 hours or until the leg joint can be moved up and down with ease. Baste frequently through the cheesecloth during the roasting period with butter and natural juices from the bottom of the pan. Remove the cheesecloth during the last 30 minutes of roasting to allow the bird to brown.

serves 12 to 15

❧ Roast Goose with Fancy Fruit Stuffing

1 fresh or thawed 7- to 10-pound goose with giblets and liver
1 medium-sized onion, sliced
1 bay leaf
1 celery stalk, chopped
3 tablespoons flour
salt to taste
freshly ground black pepper to taste
spiced crabapple slices
white grapes
Fancy Fruit Stuffing:
¼ cup butter
1 onion, finely diced
½ cup chopped celery
8 cups ½-inch stale bread cubes
½ cup black currants
3 apples, peeled, cored and diced
1 teaspoon dried sage
2 tablespoons chopped parsley
1 lemon rind, finely grated
1 cup seedless white grapes
½ cup crushed pineapple
1 teaspoon salt
1 teaspoon freshly ground black pepper
2 tablespoons lemon juice
½ cup white wine

Wash the goose in cold water, scrubbing the skin to remove any excess feathers. Wipe dry. Rub the cavity with salt and pepper and set the goose aside.

In a skillet, melt the butter. Add the onion and celery and sauté until the onion is transparent and the celery is tender.

Preheat the oven to 450°

Put the bread cubes in a large mixing bowl. Add the sautéed onion, celery and melted butter. Add the currants, apples, sage, parsley, lemon rind, grapes, pineapple, salt, pepper and lemon juice. Mix the stuffing well. Slowly pour in the wine while mixing. Use more wine if necessary to moisten the stuffing.

Fill the goose cavity about three-quarters full with the stuffing. Put any remaining stuffing under the neck skin. Sew or skewer the cavity closed and truss the goose. Place the goose on a rack in a roasting pan. Roast the goose at 450° for 10 minutes.

Reduce the oven temperature to 325° and continue to roast, allowing 20 minutes for each pound. Skim the fat from the pan periodically.

While the goose is roasting, prepare the gravy by putting the giblets and liver in a saucepan with the bay leaf, celery, and salt and pepper to taste. Add enough cold water to cover, and bring to a boil. Reduce the heat and simmer for 1½ hours.

Remove the giblets and bay leaf from the stock. Mash the onion and celery to a fine purée.

When the goose is done, place the bird on a warm platter. Spoon 4 tablespoons of the goose drippings into a small saucepan over moderate heat. Slowly sift in the flour, stirring constantly with a fork to avoid lumps. Add 4 cups of the giblet stock and continue to cook, stirring slowly, until the gravy is thickened. Season with additional salt and pepper to taste (use more flour for thicker gravy).

Garnish the goose with spiced crabapple slices and white grapes. Serve the gravy separately.

Goose was at one time a common game bird in America. Although it is still hunted, most people now get their goose, either fresh or frozen, at the butcher. Try to get a young bird or gosling, one that is under a year old and weighs 7 to 10 pounds.

serves 6 to 7

✁ Roast Stuffed Squab

6 *large squabs*
4 *tablespoons butter*
salt to taste
½ *pound scrapple*
6 *chicken livers*
½ *cup unflavored bread crumbs*
¼ *cup currants*
¼ *cup chopped onion*
3 *large white mushrooms, chopped*
6 *slices salt pork*
½ *cup brandy*
½ *cup water*

Rinse the squabs thoroughly and pat them dry. Rub them inside and out with 2 tablespoons softened butter and salt and pepper to taste.

Pour a thin layer of water into a small skillet. Add the scrapple and chicken livers and sauté for about 3 minutes. Add 2 tablespoons butter, the onion and the mushrooms, and sauté for another 5 minutes.

Preheat the oven to 350°

In a mixing bowl, combine the sautéed ingredients with the bread crumbs and currants. Season with salt and pepper to taste.

Fill the cavity of each squab with the stuffing. Place a slice of salt pork on each bird. Truss the squabs tightly.

Place the squabs in a deep roasting pan, and add the brandy and water. Roast the squabs for 50 minutes, basting frequently with the pan juices.

Remove the salt pork, and roast for another 10 to 15 minutes, or until the squabs are browned.

serves 6

✻ Roast Lamb with Dill Sauce

3 pounds breast of lamb
salt to taste
freshly ground black pepper to taste
1 carrot, chopped
1 onion, diced
3 large new potatoes, quartered
½ cup chopped celery
1½ tablespoons flour
1 tablespoon cider vinegar
1 teaspoon brown sugar
½ cup heavy cream
2 egg yolks
1 cup chopped fresh dill

Cut all excess fat from the breast of lamb. Sprinkle both sides with the salt and pepper to taste. Put the lamb into a large stew pot or Dutch oven. Add the carrot, onion, potatoes, celery, and enough water to cover. Simmer the uncovered pot over a low heat for about 1¼ hours, stirring every 20 minutes, and skimming excess fat from the top.

Drain the liquid from the pot, reserving 2 cups of it. Leave the lamb in the pot. Pour the reserved liquid into a saucepan and add the cider vinegar and brown sugar. Simmer the mixture over low heat.

Beat the cream and egg yolks together in a bowl.

Mix the flour with a little warm water in a small bowl and stir until blended.

Stir the cream mixture into the saucepan until thoroughly blended. Add the flour mixture, a little at a time, stirring until the sauce thickens (use more flour mixture for a thicker sauce). Add half the chopped dill and heat, stirring continuously, for 5 minutes. Do not let the sauce boil.

Pour the sauce over the lamb in the pot. Sprinkle the remaining dill over the top, cover and heat thoroughly before serving.

serves 4

74

✻ Lamb Stew

½ cup bacon drippings or butter
2 pounds stewing lamb, cut into 2-inch cubes
2 large onions, chopped
2 tablespoons flour
1 garlic clove, chopped
6 small white onions
½ pound baby carrots, trimmed and left whole
1 tomato, chopped
½ cup lima beans
2 bay leaves
salt to taste
freshly ground black pepper to taste

In a large, deep saucepan melt the bacon dripping. Add the meat and onions, sprinkle them with the flour, and brown well.

Add the garlic, white onions, carrots, tomato, lima beans, and bay leaves to the saucepan. Add enough water to cover.

Simmer, covered, until the meat is tender, about 1 hour. Season to taste with salt and pepper when the meat is almost cooked.

serves 4 to 6

✻ Lamb and Sausage Stew

3 fresh pork sausage links
¼ cup vegetable oil
2 large garlic cloves, finely chopped
2 pounds lamb, cubed
2 carrots, sliced
3 celery stalks, finely diced
½ teaspoon rosemary
2 teaspoons paprika
½ teaspoon salt
½ teaspoon white pepper
1½ cups beef broth
1½ cups tomato sauce

Put enough water to make a layer ½ inch deep into a skillet. Bring the water to the boil and add the sausage links. Cook until they are browned on both sides and tender.

Drain and cut the sausages into bite-sized slices.

Heat the oil and garlic in the skillet over low heat. When the garlic has browned, remove it. Add the cubed lamb and cook, stirring often, for 5 minutes. Add the carrots, celery, sausage pieces, rosemary, paprika, salt and white pepper. Cook, stirring often, until the vegetables are tender.

Add the broth and tomato sauce to the skillet and bring to a boil. Reduce the heat and simmer for 30 minutes, or until the lamb is tender when pricked with a fork. Serve over rice.

serves 6

Pot Roast

5 pounds rump roast
2 cups red wine
2 large onions, chopped
1 garlic clove, chopped
1 teaspoon salt
¼ teaspoon freshly ground black pepper
4 tablespoons olive oil
1 onion, thinly sliced
3 tomatoes, thickly sliced
6 medium-sized potatoes, peeled and cut into eighths

In a mixing bowl make a marinade by combining the wine, chopped onions, garlic, salt and pepper.

Place the meat in a large bowl and pour the marinade over it. Refrigerate the meat for 8 to 10 hours, turning it frequently.

Heat the oil in a large, heavy pot. Remove the meat from the marinade (but reserve the marinade), pat it dry, and brown it well in the hot oil.

Add the sliced onion to the pot. Add the reserved marinade and cover the pot. Cook over low heat until the meat is tender, about 3 hours.

Add the tomatoes and potatoes and cook for another 30 minutes.

The many Portuguese fishermen who came to Massachusetts contributed Mediterranean zest to New England cooking.

serves 6 to 8

Yankee Pot Roast

3 pounds bottom round, chuck or rump roast
2 tablespoons flour
½ tablespoon grated nutmeg
3 tablespoons bacon drippings, lard or butter
2 cups fresh cranberries
1 cup apple cider
2 tablespoons brown sugar
1 stick cinnamon
6 whole cloves
1 teaspoon salt

In a small bowl combine the flour and nutmeg. Rub the mixture into the meat.

In a large, heavy pot melt the bacon drippings and add the meat, browning it well on all sides.

In a saucepan combine the cranberries, apple cider, and brown sugar. Bring the mixture to a boil. Simmer over low heat until the cranberries are tender, about 8 minutes. Pour this mixture over the meat.

Put the cinnamon stick and cloves in a cheesecloth bag. Place the bag in the pot with the meat. Sprinkle the meat with the salt.

Cover the pot and simmer for 2 to 2¼ hours, or until the meat is tender. To serve, remove the spice bag and place the meat on a serving platter with the sauce.

The ingredients and style of cooking in this recipe are exactly the same as in Colonial times.

serves 6

✽ Paprika Beef

4 pounds beef round, cut into bite-sized pieces
flour for dredging
¼ cup bacon drippings or vegetable oil
2 tablespoons paprika
1 tablespoon salt
½ tablespoon freshly ground black pepper
2 tablespoons brown sugar
2 teaspoons dried mustard
½ cup lemon juice
1½ cups beef broth
4 large mushrooms, sliced
3 tablespoons flour

Dredge the beef pieces in the flour. Heat the bacon drippings in a large skillet or heavy pot and slowly brown the beef in it, a few pieces at a time.

When all of the beef is browned, return it all to the skillet or pot. Add the paprika, salt, pepper, brown sugar, mustard, lemon juice, and the beef broth. Bring the mixture to a boil, then reduce the heat, cover and simmer for 1½ hours. Add the mushrooms and onions to the beef, cover and simmer for 30 minutes longer, or until the meat is tender.

In a small bowl mix the 3 tablespoons flour with 3 tablespoons of the cooking liquid until it is evenly mixed and thin enough to pour. Pour the remaining cooking liquid from the beef into a saucepan. Stir in the flour mixture and heat, stirring continuously, until the gravy thickens.

Serve the beef and gravy over broad egg noodles.

serves 8

✽ Maple-Glazed Ham

1 5-pound cooked ham
2 tablespoons ground cloves
¾ cup pure maple syrup
¼ teaspoon dried mustard
1 cup pineapple juice
½ cup unflavored bread crumbs
¼ cup pineapple chunks, puréed
1 teaspoon brown sugar
½ teaspoon cinnamon

Cut away any brown skin from the ham. Trim the fat down to the meat all around the surface.

In a mixing bowl, mix the maple syrup, dried mustard and pineapple juice together.

Place the ham on a rack in a large roasting pan. Pour the maple syrup mixture over it.

Bake the ham in a preheated 325° oven for 1 hour, basting very generously every 10 minutes.

Mix the bread crumbs, pureed pineapple chunks, brown sugar and cinnamon together in a bowl.

Remove the ham from the oven, coat the surface with a layer of the bread crumb mixture. Baste the ham with juices from the pan to moisten the bread crumbs, and return it to the oven for another 30 minutes, basting every 10 minutes.

One of the many gifts of the Indians to the new colonists, maple syrup was the chief sweetener used in New England until the end of the nineteenth century. Make every effort to buy pure New England maple syrup. Most commercial maple syrups consist chiefly of corn syrup.

serves 8

❦ Spiced Fresh Ham

1 10-pound fresh ham
1 tablespoon ground cinnamon
1 tablespoon ground nutmeg
1 tablespoon ground ginger
1½ teaspoons salt
½ teaspoon freshly ground black pepper
6 cups white flour
1 cup warm water
2 quarts apple cider
2 eggs, beaten
3 cups unflavored bread crumbs
½ cup currant jelly

Wash the ham in warm water and dry thoroughly. In a small bowl, mix the cinnamon, nutmeg, ginger, salt and pepper together. Rub the mixture vigorously into the ham.

Put the flour into a mixing bowl. Add just enough water to form a stiff dough. Mix well. Put the dough on a lightly floured surface and roll it out to form a ¼-inch thick crust. Wrap the ham in the dough. Pinch all the edges sealed.

Preheat the oven to 325°. Place the wrapped ham, fat-side up, in a roasting pan. Pour the apple cider into the pan and bake, uncovered, for 2¼ hours, basting often.

Remove the ham from the oven. Peel off and discard the dough wrapping. Cut away and discard the ham rind.

Pour the juices from the roasting pan into a saucepan. Pour ¼ cup of the juices over the ham to moisten it, then sprinkle the ham with the bread crumbs until it is completely covered. Return the ham to the oven and bake at 325° for 20 minutes longer.

While the ham is baking again, bring the juices in the saucepan to a boil. Add the currant jelly and stir with a whisk until the gravy is smooth and well blended. Strain the gravy into a sauceboat and serve with the ham.

serves 12

❦ Ham and Apple Pie

2 pounds cooked ham, diced
5 tart apples, cored and sliced
¼ cup light brown sugar
⅛ teaspoon salt
½ teaspoon cinnamon
2 tablespoons butter
2 tablespoons lemon juice
¼ cup apple cider
1 unbaked 9-inch pastry shell

Preheat the oven to 375°.

Combine the sugar, salt, and cinnamon in a small bowl; mix well.

Butter a deep baking dish. Place alternate layers of ham and apples in the dish, sprinkling each layer with the sugar mixture and dotting each with butter. Be sure to end with a layer of apples.

Combine the lemon juice and apple cider in a small bowl. Pour over the top layer of apples. Cover the baking dish and bake in oven for 20 minutes.

At the end of 20 minutes, remove the dish from the oven and uncover it. Fit the pastry over the top of the dish. Crimp around the edge and flute. Cut a few slits in the center. Return the dish to the oven for 25 minutes longer, or until the pastry is golden.

serves 4

❦ Braised Pork Chops with Leeks

6 loin pork chops
1 tablespoon salt
½ teaspoon black pepper
¼ cup olive oil
1 cup finely chopped leeks (white parts only)
2 teaspoons chopped garlic
2 cups water
2 tablespoons dry vermouth or white vinegar

Season the pork chops on both sides with the salt and pepper.

In a heavy skillet, heat the oil. When it is hot, add the pork chops and sauté, turning occasionally, for 15 minutes or until the chops are evenly browned.

Stir in the leeks and garlic, add the water, and bring to a boil over high heat. Reduce the heat, cover the skillet, and simmer for 30 minutes, turning the chops twice.

Remove the pork chops from the skillet and place them on a serving platter. Stir the vermouth into the remaining liquid, cook for 2 minutes, and pour over the chops.

serves 6

❧ Pork Chops with Cranberries

1 tablespoon butter
6 loin pork chops, about 1 inch thick
1 teaspoon salt
freshly ground black pepper to taste
1 cup fresh or thawed cranberries
½ cup brown sugar
⅔ cup water
2 teaspoons cornstarch
1 orange, peeled and thinly sliced

Melt the butter in a heavy skillet or Dutch oven. Add the pork chops and slowly brown on both sides.

Pour off half the drippings. Sprinkle the chops with salt and pepper to taste. Add the cranberries, brown sugar and ⅓ cup of the water. Cover and simmer over medium heat for 45 minutes, or until chops are browned on the outside but pink and tender inside.

Remove the chops from the skillet and keep them in a warm oven.

Mix the cornstarch and remaining water together in a small bowl. Add the mixture to the liquid in the skillet. Cook over low heat, stirring continuously, until the sauce thickens.

Put the pork chops on a heated serving platter. Place an orange slice on each chop. Pour the sauce over the chops and serve.

serves 6

❧ Pork Chops with Apricot Stuffing

1 cup sliced dried apricots
½ cup very hot water
1 tablespoon brown sugar
6 1-inch-thick rib pork chops
¼ cup flour
salt to taste
freshly ground black pepper to taste
3 tablespoons vegetable oil
4 tablespoons butter
½ cup chopped celery
1 onion, finely diced
2 cups fine unflavored bread crumbs
1 large tart green apple, cored and diced
2 parsley sprigs, chopped
½ tablespoon dried thyme
½ tablespoon cinnamon
¼ tablespoon dried marjoram

Put the apricots, hot water and brown sugar in a bowl. Stir and let soak for 20 minutes.

Dredge the chops in the flour, coating both sides and all edges. Sprinkle with salt and pepper to taste. Heat the oil in a large skillet. Add the chops and cook until they are golden brown on both sides. Remove from the skillet and drain on paper towels.

Add the butter to the oil and drippings in the skillet. Add the celery and onion and sauté until the onion is transparent.

Add the bread crumbs, apple, parsley, thyme, cinnamon and marjoram to the skillet with the cooked vegetables. Cook over low heat, stirring constantly, for 5 minutes.

Preheat the oven to 325°.

Add the apricots and the water to the stuffing mixture. Stir until well mixed.

Spread the stuffing in a buttered baking dish or casserole. Place the pork chops on top and cover the dish with aluminum foil.

Bake for 1½ hours, or until the chops are thoroughly cooked but still tender.

serves 6

Applejack Pork Chops

2 tablespoons butter
2 tablespoons peanut or light vegetable oil
1 onion, diced
1 garlic clove, chopped
8 thinly cut pork chops
salt to taste
freshly ground black pepper to taste
¾ cup applejack or apple brandy
½ cup veal or beef broth
1½ tablespoons chopped fresh ginger
1 firm apple, cored and sliced
1 tablespoon honey
2 tablespoons applejack or apple brandy

Melt the butter and oil together in a large skillet. Add the onion and garlic and cook until the onion is translucent and slightly browned.

Remove the onion and garlic from the skillet and save. Add the pork chops to the skillet, sprinkle them with salt and pepper to taste and sauté, turning often, until they are browned and tender.

In a small saucepan, heat the ¾ cup of applejack until it is almost at a boil. Carefully light the applejack with a long match. When the flame has died, pour the applejack over the chops.

Return the onion and garlic to the skillet with the chops, and sprinkle the ginger over them. Add the broth and let simmer for around 20 minutes, or until the liquid is reduced and thickened.

While the chops are simmering in the stock, melt a pat of butter in a small skillet and add the apple slices. Cook the slices over a medium heat for about 3 minutes, or until they are tender. Add the honey and stir gently. Add the 2 tablespoons of applejack and continue to cook for another minute or so, until the honey-applejack sauce thickens slightly.

Serve the pork chops on a large platter, covered with the sauce they cooked in. Arrange the apple slices all around the chops and cover the apples with the honey sauce.

serves 4

Braised Pork Chops with Sauerkraut

1 tablespoon lard or butter
4 pork chops
2 cups sauerkraut, drained and rinsed
¼ cup chopped onion
4 tart apples, peeled, cored and sliced
4 tablespoons brown sugar
1 teaspoon caraway seeds

Melt the lard in a large skillet. Add the pork chops and slowly brown on both sides. Remove the chops from the skillet and drain off the fat.

Combine the sauerkraut, onion, apples, sugar and caraway seeds in a bowl. Pour this mixture into the skillet and place the pork chops on top of it. Cover and simmer for 45 minutes or until the chops are tender.

serves 4

❧ Smoked Pork Loaf

1 pound smoked ham, ground
1 pound ground pork
2 large eggs, beaten
½ cup light cream
½ cup coarse unflavored bread crumbs
1 teaspoon salt
freshly ground black pepper to taste
½ cup brown sugar
¼ cup honey
⅓ cup cider vinegar
⅓ cup apple cider
2 teaspoons dried mustard
½ teaspoon nutmeg
½ teaspoon ground ginger

Preheat the oven to 350°.

Put the ham, pork, eggs, cream, bread crumbs, salt and pepper into a mixing bowl and mix together thoroughly.

Put the brown sugar, honey, vinegar, cider, mustard, nutmeg and ginger into a saucepan. Bring to a boil, stirring continuously, then reduce the heat and simmer for 10 minutes.

Pour some of the liquid in the saucepan into a large round or rectangular loaf pan, enough to make a thin layer on the bottom.

Pack the meat mixture into the loaf pan. Smooth the top and bake for 45 minutes.

Baste the loaf generously with the sauce after 45 minutes of baking. Continue to bake for another 45 minutes, basting every 5 to 10 minutes.

If there is any sauce left over after basting, reheat it and pour over the loaf after it is cooked. Serve on a heated platter.

serves 8

❧ New England Salt Pork Dinner with Milk Gravy

2 pounds salt pork
water for soaking
4 tablespoons flour
2 tablespoons lard
Milk Gravy:
¼ cup fat from salt pork
3 tablespoons flour
milk divided into: 2 tablespoons, 2 tablespoons and 2 cups

Select salt pork with streaks of lean in it. Cut the pork into ½-inch slices. Soak the slices in warm water for 4 hours, changing the water 3 or 4 times.

Pat the pork slices dry. Dredge each slice in the flour.

In a skillet greased with the lard, cook the pork slowly, turning occasionally until the slices are a rich crusty brown.

To make the milk gravy, remove the slices from the skillet. Remove the skillet from the heat and drain off all but ¼ cup fat. Into this stir 3 tablespoons flour. Blend thoroughly and add 2 tablespoons milk. Stir until smooth; add 2 more tablespons milk. Mix well.

Gradually stir in 2 cups of milk. Cook over low heat, stirring constantly, until the mixture thickens. Serve the salt pork with the gravy.

serves 4

❧ Baked Venison

1 2-inch thick, top-round venison steak
2 cups flour
2 eggs, well beaten
½ teaspoon salt
½ cup water
6 bacon slices

Use a tenderizing mallet to thoroughly tenderize the venison. Score the top of the steak with a sharp knife.

In a mixing bowl make a dough of the flour, eggs, salt and water. Roll the dough out on a lightly floured surface into a thin crust large enough to wrap around the venison.

Preheat the oven to 425°.

Put the bacon slices on the crust, and place the venison on the bacon. Fold the crust over the meat so that it is covered completely. Soften the crust edges with a little warm water and seal them together.

Wrap the covered venison in heavy-duty aluminum foil, place it on a baking sheet and bake, allowing about 50 minutes for each pound of meat.

About 15 minutes before removing the venison from the oven, open and peel back the foil and raise the oven temperature to 475°. Bake for 15 minutes longer, or until the crust is golden brown.

Serve with currant or mint jelly.

serves 8

New England Boiled Dinner

5 to 6 pounds corned beef brisket
½ pound salt pork
8 carrots
8 parsnips
8 small white turnips, peeled
1 medium-sized onion
8 medium-sized potatoes
1 medium-sized head of green cabbage, cored and quartered

Place the corned beef in a large pot and add enough cold water to cover. Simmer, covered, for 2 hours. Add the salt pork and continue simmering for another 2 hours.

Skim the pot carefully and add the carrots, parsnips, turnips and onions. Cover and cook for 30 minutes.

Add the potatoes and cabbage. Cover and continue cooking until the potatoes are tender, about 30 to 40 minutes longer.

To serve, place the meat in the center of a large platter. Surround it with the drained vegetables.

serves 6 to 8

Beef and Sausage Casserole

1½ cups uncooked white rice
olive oil
1 bay leaf
¾ pound ground beef
½ pound sweet Italian sausage, chopped
1 onion, diced
1 garlic clove, finely chopped
1 medium-sized green pepper, seeded and diced
3 cups beef broth
14 ounces canned plum tomatoes
2 large eggs, beaten
4 tablespoons grated Parmesan or Romano cheese
2 tablespoons salt
½ teaspoon freshly ground black pepper
½ pound mozzarella cheese, sliced

In a large casserole or baking dish (at least 2 quarts), soak the rice in cold water for 15 minutes. Drain the rice and set the dish aside.

Heat a thin layer of olive oil in a large skillet over a low flame. Add the bay leaf, ground beef, sausage, onion, garlic, green pepper and tomatoes and cook until the meat is browned and the vegetables are tender. Remove the skillet from the heat and let cool.

Preheat the oven to 350°.

Add the beef broth and eggs to the rice in the casserole dish and mix well. Pour in the cooled meat mixture from the skillet, and add the grated cheese, salt and pepper. Stir all the ingredients until they are thoroughly mixed.

Bake for 1¾ hours.

Top the casserole with the slices of mozzarella cheese and bake for another 15 minutes, or until the cheese begins to brown.

serves 4

✂ Red Flannel Hash

1½ cups cooked chopped corned beef
1½ cups cooked chopped beets
3 cups cooked chopped potatoes
1 small onion, finely chopped
salt to taste
freshly ground black pepper to taste
1 teaspoon Worcestershire sauce
light cream or half-and-half
¼ cup bacon drippings

In a large bowl combine the corned beef, beets, potatoes, onion, salt, pepper and Worcestershire sauce with enough cream to bind the ingredients together.

Melt the bacon drippings in a skillet and spread the meat mixture evenly in the bottom. Cook over low heat. Loosen the hash around the edges with a spatula and shake the skillet occasionally to prevent the bottom from scorching. When a crust forms on the bottom, flip the hash over and brown it on the other side. Remove the hash from the skillet and serve it on a platter.

serves 4

✂ Maple Barbecue

1 4-pound spareribs rack
1 chicken, quartered, and wings separated from breasts
½ cup puréed tomatoes
½ cup lemon juice
½ cup grated onion
3 tablespoons Worcestershire sauce
½ cup pure maple syrup
salt to taste
freshly ground black pepper to taste
Tabasco sauce to taste

Line a large baking dish with aluminum foil, leaving enough extra foil on all sides to cover and seal the meat. Place the spareribs and chicken parts in the dish.

Preheat the oven to 350°.

Put the tomatoes, lemon juice, onion, Worcestershire sauce, and maple syrup in a saucepan. Season with salt, pepper and Tabasco sauce to taste. Bring the mixture quickly to a boil, then simmer, stirring, for 3 minutes.

Pour all but ¼ cup of the maple sauce over the ribs and chicken. Fold the foil over and crimp the edges sealed. Bake for 1 hour or until the ribs are fully cooked.

Remove the baking dish from the oven. Set the broiler to medium. Cut the rack of spareribs into individual rib pieces. Return the pieces to the baking dish. Brush the ribs and chicken with the remaining maple sauce and put them under the broiler. Cook, turning the ribs and chicken pieces often and basting both sides generously with the remaining maple sauce, until each part is crisp and well glazed.

To cook outdoors on an open grill, prepare the maple sauce as directed. Use the sauce as a marinade, marinating the ribs and chicken parts for 3 hours before barbecuing. Cook over hot white coals—not high flames—basting generously and often with the maple sauce.

serves 6 to 8

✂ Lamb and Apples

4 medium-sized apples, peeled, cored and halved
juice of 1 lemon
1 cup sugar
½ cup water
2 pounds breast of lamb
¼ cup honey
¼ cup lemon juice
½ teaspoon salt

Preheat the oven to 325°.

Place the apples in bowl and add enough cold water to cover. Stir in the juice of 1 lemon. Be certain the apples are covered.

In a saucepan combine the sugar and water. Simmer until the sugar is dissolved, then boil for 5 minutes. Drain the apple halves and add them to the skillet. Simmer in the syrup until glazed.

Place the lamb on a rack in a roasting dish. Bake for 1 hour. Drain off the fat and bake for 45 minutes longer. Arrange the apples around the lamb, reserving the syrup.

Combine the reserved syrup, honey, lemon juice and salt in a bowl; pour over the lamb and apples. Roast 20 minutes longer.

serves 4

✂ Boiled Leg of Lamb with Caper Sauce

1 leg of lamb, about 5 to 6 pounds
2 garlic cloves, cut into thin slivers
1 teaspoon crumbled dried rosemary
3 quarts boiling water
1 tablespoon salt
1 teaspoon black pepper
1 teaspoon dried thyme
1 onion
salt to taste
black pepper to taste
Caper Sauce:
3 tablespoons butter
3 tablespoons flour
1½ cups lamb broth
salt to taste
black pepper to taste
1 tablespoon lemon juice
½ cup drained capers

Trim the leg of lamb of excess fat. Rub it with salt and pepper. Make 10 shallow incisions in the fat side of the lamb and insert the garlic slivers.

Place the leg into a large, heavy pot containing the boiling water, 1 tablespoon salt, 1 teaspoon pepper, thyme and rosemary. Bring the water back to a boil and simmer, partially covered, until the lamb is tender and pink. Allow 12 to 15 minutes per pound once the water has resumed boiling.

When the lamb is done, transfer it to a platter and let it rest before carving. Prepare the caper sauce.

In a deep saucepan, melt the butter, then stir in the flour and cook for 3 minutes over low heat. Add the lamb broth and stir until the mixture is thickened. Season to taste. Add the lemon juice and capers and simmer for 2 minutes.

serves 6 to 8

✂ Breads ✂

The aroma of freshly baked bread warms the heart on even the gloomiest of days. Whether baked in a tin oven standing by a large open fireplace as it was centuries ago, or in today's modern oven, the effect is the same.

Commercial baking soda (called saleratus) was first introduced in 1856. Commercial yeast was first introduced in 1868. Until these two innovations became widespread, bread was made to rise either by the cook's own yeast, preserved from baking to baking, by the use of pearlash (potassium carbonate, made from wood ash), or by simply beating a lot of air into the dough. Many traditional New England bread recipes predate these easily available leavening agents. This makes them easy for today's harried cook, since they require no rising time and cook quickly.

Parker House Rolls, Boston Brown Bread, Anadama Bread, Popovers—all are New England recipes that have become all-American favorites. These and the other breads in this chapter are surprisingly easy to make. Try serving them with some of the sweet and savory jams and relishes found in the last chapter.

✂ Indian Bread

½ cup flour
1½ cups corn meal
½ teaspoon salt
4 tablespoons sugar
2 eggs, beaten
1 cup sour cream
1 teaspoon baking soda
1½ cups milk

Preheat the oven to 400°.

Combine the flour, corn meal, salt and sugar in a large bowl. Add the eggs and sour cream and beat well until smooth.

Dissolve the baking soda in the milk in a small bowl. Add to the flour mixture and mix well.

Pour the mixture into a buttered 12-inch loaf pan. Bake for 25 minutes or until a cake tester comes out clean and the bread is lightly browned.

yields 1 loaf

✂ Pumpkin Bread

½ cup vegetable oil
2 cups sugar
2 eggs
1½ cups flour
½ teaspoon salt
½ teaspoon cinnamon
2 teaspoons baking soda
1¾ cups pumpkin purée, canned or fresh
¾ cup walnuts, chopped

Preheat the oven to 350°.

Cream the oil and sugar together in a large mixing bowl. Add the eggs and beat well. Combine the flour with the salt, cinnamon and baking soda in a bowl. Add it alternately with the pumpkin purée to the creamed mixture. Stir in the nuts.

Pour the batter into two well-greased 9 × 5 × 3-inch loaf pans and bake for 1 hour, or until the loaves are browned. When done, cool the pans on racks. Cool for 15 minutes in the pan; then turn the loaves out and continue cooling.

yields 2 loaves

Cheddar Biscuits

Deep-Fried Codfish Balls

Pumpkin Pie

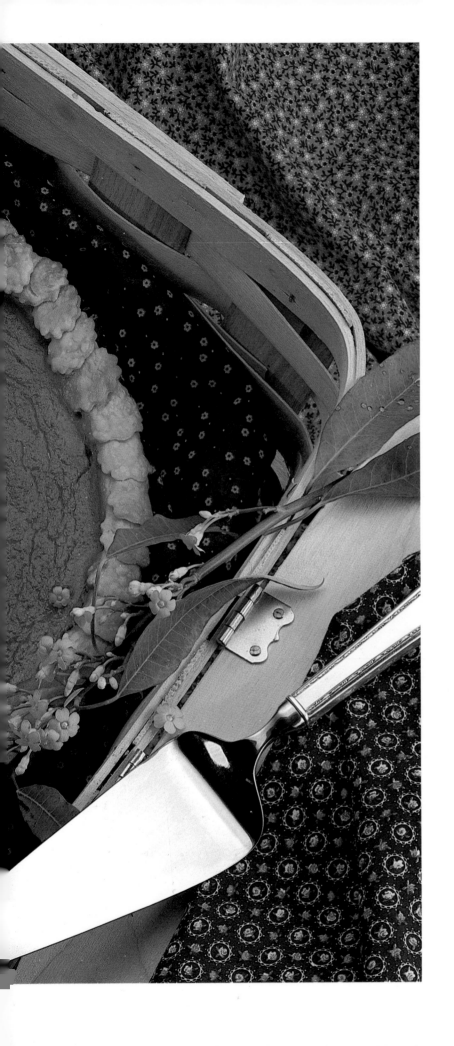

Parker House Rolls

Honey Bread

Holiday Fruitcake

Pound Cake

Apple Muffins

✻ Boston Brown Bread

1 cup rye flour
1 cup corn meal
1 cup whole wheat or graham flour
¾ teaspoon baking soda
1 teaspoon salt
¾ cup dark molasses
2 cups buttermilk
1 cup dark seedless raisins

Into a large bowl sift the rye flour, corn meal, whole wheat flour, baking soda and salt. Add the molasses, buttermilk and raisins. Stir well.

Divide the batter into 3 equal parts. Place each part into a buttered 1-pound coffee can, filling the can about three-quarters of the way full (large juice cans also work well). Cover the top of each can with buttered wax paper and then aluminum foil. Puff the foil and allow approximately 1 inch of space so that the bread has room to rise. Tie the foil and wax paper in place with string.

Place the cans on a rack set in a very large pot. Fill the pot with enough boiling water to reach three-quarters of the way up the cans. Return the water to a boil, cover the pot, reduce the heat, and steam the bread for 2½ hours. Check the pot occasionally and add water if needed to keep the water at the original level.

When the bread is done, carefully remove the cans from the pot and cool them just enough to remove the bread. Serve the bread hot with butter.

The Pilgrims used to say, "Brown bread and Gospel is good fare."

yields 3 loaves

✻ Graham Nut Bread

2 tablespoons butter, melted
½ cup sugar
½ cup molasses
2 cups buttermilk
2 teaspoons baking soda
2 cups whole wheat or graham flour
1⅔ cups white flour
1 teaspoon salt
1 teaspoon baking powder
1 cup chopped walnuts

Preheat the oven to 350°.

In a large bowl combine the butter, sugar and molasses. Mix well. Dissolve the baking soda in the buttermilk and add to the molasses mixture. Stir until well blended.

Combine the whole wheat flour, white flour, salt and baking powder in a bowl or on a large piece of waxed paper. Add to the molasses-buttermilk mixture. Add the nuts and stir well.

Pour the batter into two 9 × 5 × 3-inch greased loaf pans. Bake for about 50 minutes or until a cake tester comes out clean. Cool before serving.

The Reverend Sylvester Graham was a nineteenth-century dietary reformer. Many of his ideas are best forgotten, but his belief in the virtues of whole wheat flour is shared by many today. His name lives on in Graham crackers.

yields 2 loaves

✻ Old-Fashioned Rhode Island Johnnycakes

1 teaspoon salt
1 tablespoon butter
1 cup yellow corn meal
1 cup boiling water
¼ cup milk
2 tablespoons bacon drippings or butter

93

Preheat the oven to 475°.

Put the corn meal, salt and butter in a mixing bowl. Pour the *boiling* water over the corn meal. Stir immediately. It is crucial that the water be boiling when it is poured. Add the milk and stir until well mixed.

Melt the bacon drippings in an 8- or 9-inch round cake pan. Grease the sides of the pan and pour in the batter. Place the pan over heat until the batter begins to bubble around the edges.

Place the pan in the oven. Bake for about 30 minutes, or until golden brown. After the first 10 minutes, dot the top with butter if desired.

The name johnnycake is said by some to derive from "journey cakes," the idea being that travelers took them along. However, there is a good chance that the name comes from the Indians who taught the settlers how to cook corn meal—the Shawnees.

serves 6

✳ Anadama Bread

½ cup corn meal
3 tablespoons butter
¼ cup dark molasses
2 teaspoons salt
¾ cup boiling water
1 package active dry yeast
¼ cup warm water
1 egg, beaten
3 cups flour

In a large bowl combine the corn meal, butter, molasses, salt and boiling water. Mix well. Let the mixture stand at room temperature until it is lukewarm.

Dissolve the yeast in 3 tablespoons of luke-warm water in a small bowl. Stir it into the corn meal mixture. Stir in the egg and 1½ cups flour. Beat well. Stir in the remaining 1½ cups flour and mix until the dough forms a soft ball. Use your hands to mix the dough if it is easier.

Place the dough in a greased 9 × 5 × 3-inch loaf pan. Cover it with a clean cloth and set it in a warm place until the dough doubles in bulk, about 1 to 1½ hours. Sprinkle the top of the loaf with a little corn meal and salt. Bake in a 350° oven for 50 to 55 minutes. Cool completely before slicing.

Stories about the origin of Anadama bread abound. One of the more plausible is that Anna, a fine but temperamental cook, left her husband. He had to make her bread recipe himself, muttering all the time, "Anna, damn her."

yields 1 loaf

✳ Honey Bread

1¼ cups milk
2 teaspoons salt
4 tablespoons butter
¼ cup honey
¼ cup sugar
2 packages active dry yeast
½ cup lukewarm water
¼ teaspoon sugar
1 large egg
5 cups flour

In a large saucepan combine the milk, salt, butter, honey and ¼ cup sugar. Cook over low heat until the butter is completely melted.

In a small bowl, dissolve the yeast in the water with ¼ teaspoon sugar. Add the yeast to the heated milk mixture. Add the egg and flour and combine thoroughly.

Turn the dough out on to a lightly floured surface and knead for 10 minutes. Place the dough in a large greased bowl. Cover with a clean cloth and place the bowl in the cold oven with a bowl of hot water underneath. Let the dough rise until it is doubled in bulk, about 1 hour.

Remove the dough from the oven and divide it in half. Knead each half for 1 minute. Place the halves into greased 9 × 5 × 3-inch loaf pans. Place the pans in the cold oven with a bowl of hot water underneath until the dough rises above the edge of the pans. This should take about 1 hour.

Bake at 350° for 30 minutes or until the bread is lightly browned, firm to the touch, and sounds hollow when tapped. Cool thoroughly before slicing.

yields 2 loaves

✂ Old-Fashioned Raisin Bread

1 cup dark seedless raisins
1 teaspoon baking soda
1 cup boiling water
1½ cups flour
½ cup sugar
½ teaspoon salt
1 egg
½ teaspoon pure vanilla extract
1 tablespoon vegetable oil

Preheat the oven to 350°.

Combine the raisins and baking soda in a mixing bowl. Add the boiling water, cover, and set aside until cool, about 1 hour.

In a medium-sized mixing bowl stir together the flour, sugar and salt. Add the raisins and their liquid and the egg, vanilla extract and oil. Stir until well mixed.

Pour the batter into a greased and floured 9 × 5 × 3-inch loaf pan and bake for 35 to 45 minutes, or until the bread is lightly browned and firm to the touch.

yields 1 loaf

✂ Cranberry-Nut Loaf

3 cups flour
4 teaspoons baking powder
¼ cup sugar
1 teaspoon salt
½ cup chopped walnuts
1 egg
1 cup milk
2 tablespoons melted butter
1 cup cranberries
¼ cup sugar
1 teaspoon pure almond or vanilla extract

Preheat the oven to 350°.

In a large bowl, mix the flour with the baking powder, ¼ cup sugar and salt. Add the walnuts and mix lightly.

In a small mixing bowl beat the egg. Add the milk and butter and mix well.

Chop the cranberries finely and mix them with ¼ cup sugar. Add the cranberries and the almond or vanilla extract to the egg mixture.

Stir the flour mixture into the egg-cranberry mixture. Mix until well blended. Pour the batter into a buttered 9 × 5 × 3-inch loaf pan. Bake for 1 hour or until the bread tests done with a cake tester. When done, remove from oven and cool the pan on a rack for 10 minutes; turn the loaf out and continue to cool on rack.

yields 1 loaf

❧ Corn Muffins

2 cups yellow corn meal
1 teaspoon salt
2 cups boiling water
1 cup cold milk
2 eggs, beaten
4 teaspoons baking powder
2 tablespoons melted butter

Preheat the oven to 375°.

Combine the corn meal and salt in a mixing bowl.

Pour the *boiling* water over the corn meal. Stir immediately. It is crucial that the water be boiling when it is poured.

Add the milk immediately. Add the eggs and stir well. Mix in the baking powder and butter. Stir well.

Pour the batter into greased muffin pans. Bake for 20 to 25 minutes or until the muffins are golden brown. Serve warm.

yields 12 muffins

❧ Acorn Squash Muffins

2 cups flour
2 teaspoons baking powder
½ teaspoon salt
½ cup sugar
¼ teaspoon cinnamon
¼ teaspoon grated nutmeg
1 egg, beaten
1 cup mashed acorn squash
1 cup milk

Preheat the oven to 400°

In a large mixing bowl combine the flour, baking powder, salt, sugar, cinnamon and nutmeg.

In another bowl beat the egg. Add the squash and milk and blend well.

Add the squash mixture to the dry ingredients and stir just until the mixtures are combined.

Fill the cups of greased muffin pans three-quarters full. Bake for 20 to 25 minutes. Serve hot or cold with butter.

makes approximately 18 muffins

❧ Apple Muffins

4 tablespoons butter, softened
2 cups flour
4 teaspoons baking powder
¼ teaspoon baking soda
½ teaspoon grated nutmeg
½ teaspoon salt
¼ cup sugar
2 eggs
1 cup sour cream
1½ cups chopped apple

Preheat the oven to 425°.

Grease the muffin pans and set them aside.

In a large bowl combine the flour, baking powder, baking soda, nutmeg and salt.

In another large mixing bowl, cream the butter and sugar until the mixture is light and fluffy. Beat in the eggs, 1 at a time. Add the flour mixture, 1 cup at a time, beating it in alternately with the sour cream. End with the sour cream.

Stir the chopped apples into the mixture. Spoon the batter into the muffin pans, filling each cup about halfway. Bake for 15 to 20 minutes or until a cake tester comes out clean. Serve hot.

makes approximately 16 muffins

✂ Cheddar Biscuits

1 cup flour
¼ teaspoon salt
⅓ cup butter
1 cup grated Cheddar cheese

Preheat oven to 350°.

Combine the flour and salt in a large bowl. Cut in the butter with a pastry blender or two knives. Add the cheese and mix lightly with your hands until the dough holds together.

Roll the dough out about ½-inch thick on a lightly floured surface. Cut out biscuits with a small, greased biscuit cutter. Prick the tops of the biscuits with a fork.

Place the biscuits on an ungreased cookie sheet and bake for 12 to 15 minutes or until the biscuits are a rich Cheddar color, but not brown. Cool before serving.

makes approximately 24 biscuits

✂ Parker House Rolls

½ cup scalded milk
½ cup boiling water
1 teaspoon salt
1 tablespoon butter
1 teaspoon sugar
1 package active dry yeast dissolved in ¼ cup
   lukewarm water
3 cups flour
½ cup melted butter

Preheat the oven to 400°

Place the milk, water, salt, butter and sugar in a mixing bowl and mix well. Add the yeast mixture. Add the flour and mix until the dough is stiff enough to knead. Cover the dough with a clean cloth and let it rise until doubled in bulk, about 20 minutes.

Shape the dough into 24 balls and put them on buttered cookie sheets or in muffin pans. Cover with a clean cloth and let rise in a warm place or until doubled in bulk, about 15 to 20 minutes.

Flour the handle of a wooden spoon and press it against each of the balls until they are almost cut in half.

Brush one half of each ball with melted butter. Fold over the other half and press the halves together. Let the dough rise once more for 15 to 20 minutes.

Bake for 15 minutes or until golden. Brush the tops with butter after baking. Serve warm.

The Parker House hotel was opened in Boston in 1855. Its dining room soon became known as one of the best places in the city to eat. These rolls were created there.

yields 24 rolls

✂ Popovers

1 cup flour
½ teaspoon salt
2 to 3 eggs, beaten (use 3 eggs if they are small)
1 cup milk
1 tablespoon melted butter
butter

Preheat the oven to 450°.

Combine all the ingredients in a large mixing bowl. Beat with a spoon or mix in a blender until the batter is completely smooth.

Fill each cup in a well-buttered preheated muffin pan one-third full. Bake the popovers for 15 minutes. Reduce the heat to 350° and continue baking for 20 to 25 minutes. Serve hot with butter.

Popovers pop when the steam that forms inside them expands as they cook. If your popovers don't pop, it is probably because the oven isn't hot enough or the batter doesn't have enough eggs in it.

makes 12 popovers

Date Nut Bread

1 cup buttermilk
1 egg, slightly beaten
2 tablespoons butter
½ cup firmly packed light brown sugar
1 cup flour
1 teaspoon baking soda
½ teaspoon salt
1 cup rolled oats
1 cup chopped dates
½ cup chopped walnuts

Preheat the oven to 325°.

In a large bowl combine the eggs, buttermilk and butter. Mix until well blended. Add the brown sugar and stir well.

In a bowl combine the flour with the baking soda and salt. Add the rolled oats and mix gently.

Stir the flour and oats into the egg mixture and mix well. Add the dates and nuts. Mix well.

Turn the batter into a greased 9 × 5 × 3-inch loaf pan. Bake for 1¼ hours.

Remove from oven to a cooling rack. Cool in the pan for 10 minutes. Turn out onto the rack and cool completely.

makes 1 loaf

Cornsticks

½ cup flour
1 teaspoon baking soda
1 teaspoon baking powder
2 teaspoons sugar
1½ cups corn meal
2 eggs, beaten
2 cups buttermilk
3 tablespoons melted butter

Preheat the oven to 425°.

In a large bowl combine the flour, baking soda, salt, baking powder and sugar. Stir in corn meal.

In another bowl combine the eggs, buttermilk and melted butter. Add to the flour mixture and beat well.

Butter the molds of a 12-stick cast-iron cornstick pan. Spoon the batter into the molds, filling them two-thirds full.

Bake for 20 to 25 minutes or until golden brown. Serve at once.

makes 12 cornsticks

Buttermilk Biscuits

2 cups flour
1 teaspoon baking powder
½ teaspoon baking soda
1 teaspoon salt
4 tablespoons softened butter
1 cup thick buttermilk

Sift the flour, baking powder, baking soda and salt into a mixing bowl. Cut in the butter with a pastry blender or two knives until the mixture resembles a coarse meal. Add just enough of the buttermilk to make a soft dough. Mix lightly.

Turn the dough out onto a lightly floured surface. Knead for about 5 minutes.

Preheat the oven to 450°.

Roll out the dough on a floured surface to ½-inch thickness. Cut biscuits from the dough with a 2-inch floured biscuit cutter.

Place the biscuits on lightly greased baking sheets. Bake for 10 to 12 minutes. Serve hot.

makes 12 to 14 biscuits

❧ New England Griddlecakes

2 cups flour
4 teaspoons baking powder
½ teaspoon salt
2 tablespoons sugar
2 eggs
1¾ cups milk
2 tablespoons butter

In a large mixing bowl combine the flour, baking powder, salt and sugar.

Beat the eggs in another large bowl and add it to the egg and milk mixture. Blend in the dry ingredients. Stir gently only until the ingredients are well mixed. Do not over beat.

Heat an ungreased griddle over medium-high heat. Drop the batter from a large spoon onto the griddle. Cook about 1 minute on each side. The cakes will bubble on top and be dry around the edges; they are ready to be turned at this point.

Remove the cakes from the griddle when done and continue making griddlecakes until the batter is gone. Serve hot with butter and pure maple syrup.

makes approximately 18 cakes

❧ Old-Fashioned Oatmeal Bread

¾ cup milk
1 package active dry yeast
1 cup quick-cooking oatmeal
1½ teaspoons salt
½ cup molasses
1 tablespoon melted butter
5 cups flour
melted butter

Heat the milk in a saucepan until a thin skin forms on top. Remove the saucepan from the heat and skim.

When the milk has cooled to lukewarm, stir in the yeast.

In a large mixing bowl combine the oatmeal, boiling water, salt, molasses and melted butter. Stir to mix well. Cool to lukewarm. Stir in the flour and the milk and yeast mixture. Mix thoroughly with your hands.

Cover the bowl with a clean towel and let stand in a warm place until the dough is doubled in bulk, about 1½ hours.

Turn the dough out onto a lightly floured surface and knead gently for 3 minutes. Divide the dough in half and shape each half into a loaf. Place into 2 buttered 9 × 5 × 3-inch loaf pans and cover with clean towels. Let the dough rise until doubled in bulk, about 50 to 60 minutes.

Preheat the oven to 350°.

Bake the loaves for 1 hour or until well browned. Remove from the oven and brush tops with melted butter. Cool in the pans for 15 minutes. Turn out onto cooling racks and cool completely.

makes 2 loaves

❧ Desserts ❧

Homemade desserts are an important part of the New England culinary tradition. That tradition continues today, in part because independent New Englanders refuse to rely on a store or bakery to provide them with their sweets.

Some of America's favorite desserts originate in New England. Apple Pandowdy, sometimes called Apple Brown Betty, is made now in a style very close to that of Colonial times. Beloved cookies with whimsical names like Joe Froggers, Hermits and Snickerdoodles also come from New England, although other parts of the country would like to claim them. And Toll House Cookies, the original chocolate-chip cookies, are named for the famous Toll House Inn in Massachusetts.

New Englanders made the best of what native ingredients they had in the early days. Included in this chapter are recipes for Maple Syrup Cake, Maple Nut Frosting, two kinds of pumpkin pie, Indian Pudding and Cranberry Snow. Many require brown sugar, maple syrup or molasses for sweetening, a reminder of the days when refined white sugar was an expensive luxury.

❧ Wellesley Fudge Cake

4 squares unsweetened chocolate
½ cup hot water
½ cup sugar
2 cups flour
1 teaspoon baking soda
1 teaspoon salt
½ cup butter
1¼ cups sugar
3 eggs
1 teaspoon pure vanilla extract
⅔ cup milk

Preheat the oven to 350°.

Combine the chocolate and hot water in the top of a double boiler. Cook over hot, not boiling, water until the chocolate is melted. Add ½ cup sugar and cook for 2 minutes longer. Set aside.

On to a large piece of wax paper sift the flour, baking soda and salt. Sift together twice more and set aside.

Cream the butter in a mixing bowl. Add 1¼ cups sugar and cream together until light and fluffy. Add the eggs, 1 at a time, beating well after each addition. Add the vanilla extract. Add the flour alternately with the milk, beating well after each addition. Begin and end with the flour. Add the chocolate mixture and blend well.

Pour the batter into 2 greased and floured 9-inch square cake pans. Bake for 25 to 30 minutes or until a cake tester inserted into the center comes out clean. Cool the pans on racks for 10 minutes, then turn them out and continue to cool. When cool, frost the cakes with Fudge Frosting (see below).

Named for the famed New England women's college, this cake was served in village tearooms on Wellesley Square.

serves 8 to 10

❧ Fudge Frosting

4 squares unsweetened chocolate
1½ cups milk
4 cups sugar
⅛ teaspoon salt
4 teaspoons light corn syrup
¼ cup butter
2 teaspoons pure vanilla extract

Place the chocolate and milk in a heavy saucepan. Cook over low heat, stirring constantly, until well blended.

Add the sugar, salt and corn syrup. Stir until the sugar is dissolved. Boil the mixture over very low heat, stirring occasionally, until small amounts dropped into cold water form soft balls. This will be when the mixture is approximately 234° to 240° on a candy thermometer.

Remove the saucepan from the heat. Add the butter and vanilla extract and mix well. Cool the mixture to lukewarm and then beat it until creamy.

To frost the Wellesley Fudge Cake, place one layer top-side down on a cake plate. Spread with approximately one-third of the frosting. Place the second layer on top, right-side up, and frost the sides with approximately one-third the frosting. Then frost the top of the cake with the remaining frosting. Smooth the frosting and swirl it with a knife. Let the frosting set before cutting the cake.

❧ Maple Syrup Cake

⅓ cup butter
½ cup sugar
¾ cup pure maple syrup
2¼ cups flour
1 tablespoon baking powder
½ teaspoon salt
⅓ cup milk
3 egg whites
1 teaspoon pure vanilla extract

Preheat the oven to 350°.

In a mixing bowl cream the butter and sugar together until light and fluffy. Add the maple syrup and mix well.

Combine the flour, baking powder and salt in a bowl. Add the mixture alternately with the milk to the butter mixture.

In a separate bowl beat the egg whites until they are stiff but not dry. Fold them into the batter. Add the vanilla extract and mix gently.

Pour the batter into a greased 9 × 5 × 3-inch loaf pan and bake for 35 minutes or until a cake tester inserted into the center comes out clean. Cool the cake in the pan on a rack for 15 minutes. Turn the cake out on to the rack and continue cooling.

When the cake is cool, frost it with Maple Nut Frosting (see below).

serves 8

❧ Maple Nut Frosting

1 cup sugar
1 cup pure maple syrup
⅓ cup water
¼ teaspoon cream of tartar
1 egg white
½ cup chopped nuts

Place the sugar, maple syrup, water and cream of tartar in a saucepan. Cook over medium heat, stirring constantly, until the mixture spins a thread when dropped from spoon.

Beat the egg white in a mixing bowl until it is stiff but not dry. Pour the sugar mixture slowly over the egg white, beating constantly. Continue to beat the mixture until it is of spreading consistency.

Fold in the nuts and spread the frosting on the cake.

Desserts

✄ Holiday Fruitcake

1 pound seedless dark raisins
1 pound seedless light raisins
1 pound currants
1 cup almonds
1 cup pecans
juice of ½ orange
grated rind of ½ orange
2 tablespoons butter, softened
1 cup butter
1½ cups sugar
6 eggs, separated
2 tablespoons pure maple syrup
2 cups flour
1 tablespoon brandy
⅛ teaspoon cinnamon
¼ teaspoon ground cloves
¼ teaspoon ground ginger
¼ teaspoon grated nutmeg

Chop the dark raisins, light raisins, currants, almonds and pecans finely and mix together in a bowl. Dredge with 2 tablespoons flour. Set aside.

Line a 9-inch ring-mold cake pan with wax paper. Butter the paper and sprinkle it with flour. Set aside.

Preheat the oven to 250°.

In a mixing bowl beat the butter until creamy. Add the sugar and beat until light, about 2 minutes. Add the egg yolks and beat until fluffy.

In a separate bowl, beat the egg whites until they are stiff but not dry. Fold the egg whites into the butter yolk. Add the maple syrup.

Little by little, add the flour to the mixture. Beat well after each addition. Add the brandy and beat well. Next add the cinnamon, cloves, ginger, nutmeg and fruit and nut mixture. Mix well. Pour into the cake mold.

Place the mold in a pan of water in the oven. Cover until the last half hour of baking, then uncover. Bake 4 hours or until a cake tester or toothpick comes out clean. Remove the cake and cool it completely. Wrap the fruit cake closely in aluminum foil and put in a cool place until ready to use. Every 3 to 4 weeks, pour 2 ounces of Bourbon whiskey onto the cake to mellow it. This cake will keep for 9 months to 1 year, getting better all the time. Serve cut very thin.

serves 10 or more

✄ Toll House Cookies

½ cup butter
½ cup sugar
¼ cup firmly packed light brown sugar
1 egg, beaten
1 teaspoon pure vanilla extract
1 cup flour
½ teaspoon baking soda
½ cup chopped walnuts or pecans
6 ounces semisweet chocolate bits

Preheat the oven to 375°.

In a large mixing bowl cream the butter until soft. Gradually beat in the sugar and brown sugar, beating well after each addition. Beat in the egg and vanilla extract.

Add the flour and baking soda to the mixture. Stir until smooth. Stir in the nuts and chocolate bits, making sure they are evenly distributed throughout the batter.

Drop the batter by scant teaspoons 2 inches apart onto lightly greased cookie sheets. Bake for 8 to 10 minutes or until the edges begin to brown. Cool on racks.

The famous Toll House Inn in Massachusetts was established by Ruth Wakefield. This is her personal recipe.

Makes 48 cookies

102

❧ Joe Froggers

1 cup butter
2 cups sugar
1 tablespoon salt
¾ cup water
¼ cup dark rum
2 teaspoons baking soda
2 cups dark molasses
7 cups flour
1 tablespoon ground ginger
1 teaspoon grated nutmeg
½ teaspoon ground cloves

Cream the butter and sugar together in a mixing bowl until light and fluffy.

In a small bowl dissolve the salt in the water and mix in the rum.

In another small bowl, add the baking soda to the molasses.

Combine the flour, ginger, cloves and nutmeg. Add the flour mixture alternately with the liquid ingredients to the creamed butter and sugar. Stir well between additions. The dough will be sticky. Chill overnight in refrigerator.

Preheat the oven to 375°.

Flour a work surface and rolling pin. Roll the dough out to ½-inch thickness. Cut it into circles or shapes with a large cookie cutter. Place the cookies 2 inches apart on greased cookie sheets. Bake for 10 to 12 minutes or until golden. Cool on racks.

makes 48 to 60 cookies

❧ Coconut Jumbles

⅔ cup butter
1 cup sugar
1 egg, beaten
1 cup flour
1 cup freshly grated coconut

Preheat the oven to 375°. Heavily grease two baking sheets and set aside.

Cream the butter in a large mixing bowl. Add the sugar and continue creaming until the mixture is light and fluffy. Add the egg and mix well. Stir in the flour and mix well. Gradually add the coconut and mix until the batter is stiff.

Drop the batter by well-rounded teaspoons onto the baking sheets. Bake 5 to 7 minutes or until lightly browned. Cool for 30 seconds on the baking sheets and then remove to cooling racks. Cool completely.

makes approximately 36 cookies

❧ Hermits

½ cup sugar
⅓ cup butter
1 egg
3 cups flour
½ teaspoon salt
1 teaspoon cinnamon
½ teaspoon grated nutmeg
½ cup dark molasses
½ cup cup buttermilk
1 cup raisins

Preheat the oven to 350°.

In a mixing bowl cream the sugar and butter until light and fluffy. Beat in the egg.

Combine the flour, salt, cinnamon and nutmeg in a small bowl. Mix the molasses with the buttermilk in another small bowl. Add the molasses mixture alternately with the flour mixture to the creamed sugar and butter. Stir in the raisins.

Drop the dough by teaspoons approximately 1 inch apart on to a greased cookie sheet. Bake for 8 to 10 minutes, or until lightly browned. Cool on a rack.

makes 72 cookies

✂ Snickerdoodles

2 eggs
2 cups water
½ cup butter, softened
1 teaspoon pure vanilla extract
4 cups flour
4 teaspoons baking powder
1 teaspoon salt
1 cup milk
1 cup raisins, chopped
1 tablespoon sugar
1 teaspoon cinnamon

Preheat the oven to 350°.

Beat the eggs in a mixing bowl, gradually adding the sugar. Stir in the butter and add the vanilla.

Combine the flour, baking powder and salt in a bowl. Add the flour mixture alternately with the milk to the egg mixture. Beat well after each addition. Stir in the raisins. Drop the dough by teaspoons about 1 inch apart on to greased cookie sheets. Combine 1 tablespoon sugar and the cinnamon in a small bowl. Sprinkle the mixture generously over the cookies. Bake for 20 minutes or until cookies are golden. Cool on racks.

makes 36 cookies

✂ Oatmeal Cookies

1 egg, beaten
½ cup sugar
¼ cup melted butter
¼ cup melted lard
2 teaspoons molasses
2 teaspoons milk
1 cup rolled oats (not instant oatmeal)
¼ cup raisins
¼ cup chopped nuts
¾ cup flour
½ teaspoon cinnamon
¼ teaspoon baking soda
¼ teaspoon salt

Preheat the oven to 325°.

In a large mixing bowl combine the egg, sugar, melted butter, melted lard, molasses and milk. Mix well.

In another bowl combine the oats, flour, cinnamon, baking soda and salt. Stir in the raisins and the nuts. Add to the egg and sugar mixture and combine until well blended.

Drop the dough by heaping teaspoons about 2 inches apart on to greased baking sheets. Bake for 10 to 12 minutes or until browned. Cool cookies on racks.

makes 36 cookies

✂ Gingersnaps

4 cups flour
½ cup sugar
½ teaspoon salt
1 teaspoon ground ginger
½ cup butter
½ cup lard
1 teaspoon baking soda
1 tablespoon hot water
1 cup molasses

Preheat the oven to 350°.

Combine the sugar, salt and ginger in a large mixing bowl. Cut in the butter and lard with a pastry blender, two knives, or your fingers. Blend until the particles are like coarse crumbs.

Dissolve the baking soda in the water. Make a well in the center of the flour mixture and pour in the hot water and molasses. Mix well.

Form the dough into a ball and wrap it in aluminum foil. Chill thoroughly in refrigerator. Cut the dough into slices ½ inch thick.

Place the slices 2 inches apart on a greased cookie sheet. Bake for 5 to 7 minutes. Cool on a rack.

makes 60 cookies

✂ Plain Pastry

2 cups flour
½ teaspoon salt
¾ cup butter, lard or solid vegetable shortening
4 tablespoons cold water

Sift the flour with salt into a large mixing bowl. Cut in the shortening with a pastry blender, two knives, or your fingertips until the mixture is crumbly.

Sprinkle the cold water over the flour mixture. Mix lightly with a fork until the dough holds together. Press the dough lightly into a ball. Chill in the refrigerator for at least 1 hour.

Roll the dough out on a lightly floured surface. Line a 9-inch pie plate with half the dough; trim the pastry so that ½ inch hangs over the edge. Use the other half of the dough for the top crust or for an additional pie. Bake according to the instructions in the particular recipe.

If you do not need two crusts, either halve the recipe or make both crusts and freeze one for later use.

makes enough pastry for 1 2-crust 9-inch pie

✂ Blueberry Pie

1 quart fresh blueberries
1 cup sugar
1 tablespoon flour
¼ teaspoon grated nutmeg
2 tablespoons butter, cut up
2 pastries for 9-inch pies

Preheat the oven to 450°

Wash the blueberries and drain them well.

Line a pie pan with one of the pastries, trimming so that about ½ inch hangs over the edge. Reserve the second pastry for the top of the pie.

Mix 1 tablespoon sugar with the flour and sprinkle the mixture into the pie crust. Fill the crust with the blueberries and sprinkle them with the nutmeg. Sprinkle the blueberries with the remaining sugar and dot with butter.

Place the second pastry over the top to cover the blueberries. Tuck the top crust under the overlap of the bottom crust and seal by crimping the edges firmly together. Prick the top of pie with a fork to let steam escape.

Place the pie on the lowest shelf of the oven for 10 minutes. Then move it to the middle shelf and lower the heat to 350°. Continue baking for 30 minutes or until the crust is golden.

serves 8

✂ Pumpkin Pie I

1 cup pumpkin purée, fresh or canned
3 eggs, separated
½ cup sugar
¾ cup milk
2 tablespoons melted butter
½ teaspoon salt
½ teaspoon ground ginger
¼ teaspoon grated nutmeg
1 teaspoon cinnamon
1 tablespoon unflavored gelatin
¼ cup cold water
½ cup sugar
1 pastry for 9-inch pie

Preheat the oven to 450°.

Fit the pastry into a 9-inch pie pan and crimp it around the edges. Prick the pastry all over with a fork and bake for 10 minutes or until golden brown. When done, remove from oven and let cool.

Place the pumpkin purée in the top of a double boiler. Beat the egg yolks and add them to the pumpkin. Add ½ cup sugar and the milk, butter, salt, ginger, nutmeg and cinnamon. Cook, stirring constantly, until mixture thickens and reaches the consistency of custard. Remove from heat.

Soften the gelatin in cold water. Combine the gelatin with the pumpkin mixture and stir until dissolved. Chill until slightly thickened.

In a small bowl, beat the egg whites until they are stiff but not dry. Gradually beat in ½ cup sugar. Fold into the pumpkin mixture.

Pour the mixture into the pastry shell. Chill for 3 hours or until firm. Serve with whipped cream.

serves 8

Pumpkin Pie II

3 eggs, beaten
1 cup sugar
½ teaspoon salt
1 teaspoon cinnamon
½ teaspoon ground ginger
½ teaspoon grated nutmeg
2 tablespoons brandy
2 cups milk
3 cups pumpkin purée, fresh or canned
3 pastries for 9-inch pies

Preheat the oven to 375°.

In a large bowl mix the beaten eggs, sugar, salt, cinnamon, ginger, nutmeg, milk, and brandy. Stir well.

To this mixture add the pumpkin. Stir until thoroughly combined.

Pour the pumpkin mixture into 3 pie plates lined with the pastries and bake for 40 to 45 minutes, or until a knife inserted halfway comes out clean. Cool before serving.

makes 3 pies

Early American Apple Pie

6 to 8 apples, peeled, cored, and thinly sliced
¼ cup sugar
¾ cup gingersnap crumbs
1 tablespoon flour
½ teaspoon cinnamon
⅛ teaspoon nutmeg
¼ teaspoon salt
½ cup chopped walnuts
¼ cup melted butter
½ cup pure maple syrup
1 pastry for 9-inch pie

Preheat the oven to 350°.

Fit the pastry into a 9-inch pie pan. Arrange half the sliced apples in the pastry shell.

In a mixing bowl combine the sugar, gingersnap crumbs, flour, cinnamon, salt, nutmeg, walnuts and butter. Blend well.

Sprinkle half of the crumb mixture over the apples in the pie shell. Place the remaining apple slices in a layer over the crumb mixture. Sprinkle with the remaining crumb mixture.

Bake the pie for 45 minutes. Heat the maple syrup to boiling and pour it evenly over the pie. Bake 15 to 20 minutes longer or until the apples are tender.

serves 6

✺ New England Pie

4 eggs
½ cup brown sugar
½ teaspoon salt
½ teaspoon cinnamon
⅓ cup melted butter
1 cup pure maple syrup
1 cup whole pecans
1 9-inch pie shell

Preheat the oven to 375°.

Combine the eggs, sugar, salt, cinnamon, butter and maple syrup in a mixing bowl. Beat well with an electric blender. When blended together, mix in the pecans and pour the mixture into the pie shell.

Bake for 15 minutes. Reduce the heat to 325° and bake for 30 minutes or until the filling is firm and the crust is golden-brown.

serves 6

✺ Apple Pandowdy

1½ cups flour
¼ teaspoon salt
½ cup butter
ice water
¼ cup melted butter
Apple filling:
½ cup sugar
½ teaspoon cinnamon
¼ teaspoon salt
¼ teaspoon grated nutmeg
10 large apples, peeled, cored, and thinly sliced
½ cup Vermont maple syrup
3 tablespoons melted butter
¼ cup water

Combine the flour and salt in a large bowl. Cut in the butter with a pastry blender or two knives until the mixture is crumb-like. Sprinkle with just enough ice water to hold the mixture together.

Roll the dough out on a floured surface and brush it with the melted butter. Cut the dough in half. Stack the halves on top of each other and cut them in half again. Brush the pieces with melted butter. Cut them in half again. Brush the pieces with the melted butter. Cut the pieces in half yet again. There should now be 16 equal pieces. Brush all the pieces with butter again and stack them on top of each other. Wrap them with plastic wrap and chill for at least 1 hour.

Roll the stacked pastry pieces out as if they were a single piece of dough. Divide it into half. Use one portion to line a greased, deep, medium-sized baking dish. Roll out and reserve the other portion for the top. Refrigerate the lined dish and the remaining dough while you make the filling.

Preheat the oven to 400°.

To make the filling, combine the sugar, cinnamon, salt and nutmeg in a large bowl. Add the apple slices to the bowl and coat them thoroughly with the sugar mixture. Put the apple slices into the pastry-lined baking dish.

In a small bowl combine the maple syrup with the melted butter and water. Pour the mixture over the apples. Cover the pan with the reserved pastry and crimp the edges together. Place in the oven for 10 minutes; then reduce heat to 325°. At this time, make slits in the top crust with a sharp knife. Return to oven and bake for 1 hour. Serve hot with heavy cream.

serves 6 to 8

❧ Apple Fritters

½ cup flour
½ cup sugar
⅛ teaspoon salt
2 teaspoons baking powder
2 eggs
½ cup milk
½ cup light cream
2 cups finely chopped tart apple
oil for frying
confectioner's sugar

In a mixing bowl combine the flour, sugar, salt and baking powder. Beat in the eggs, milk and light cream. Continue beating until the batter is smooth. Stir in the chopped apples.

Heat the oil in a deep skillet until it is hot, about 370° to 375° on a deep-fat thermometer. Drop the batter by teaspoons into the oil and fry until the fritters are lightly golden brown. Drain on paper towels and sprinkle with confectioner's sugar. Serve with maple syrup or honey.

serves 6

❧ Apple Cobbler

2 cups thinly sliced apples
½ cup brown sugar
¼ teaspoon almond extract
½ teaspoon pure vanilla extract
½ teaspoon cinnamon
1½ cups sifted flour
3 tablespoons baking powder
2 tablespoons honey
½ teaspoon salt
⅓ cup vegetable shortening
½ cup milk
1 beaten egg

Lightly butter a medium-sized pan. Arrange the apple slices in layers in the pan. Preheat the oven to 400°.

Mix the brown sugar, almond extract, vanilla extract and cinnamon together in a small bowl. Sprinkle the mixture over the apples. Put the pan into the oven.

Sift the flour, baking powder and salt together in a bowl. Blend in the honey and shortening with your fingers until the mixture is coarse and grainy. Add the egg and slowly mix in the milk to moisten the dough.

With your fingers spread the dough into a sheet large enough to cover the apple. Lay the dough over the hot apples. Sprinkle with some brown sugar. Return the pan to the oven and bake for 40 minutes longer.

serves 8

❧ Doughnuts

1 scant cup milk
⅓ cup sugar
1 egg, beaten
4 tablespoons butter
½ teaspoon baking powder
1 to 1½ cups flour
lard for frying

In a large bowl combine the milk, sugar, egg, butter, baking powder and flour. Mix together well, knead gently, and add more flour if necessary. Knead about 8 times and then roll the dough out on to a lightly floured surface. Cut the dough with a doughnut cutter.

Heat the lard to 370° in a deep skillet. Add the doughnuts and fry on both sides until they are brown and light. Drain the doughnuts on paper towels; sprinkle them with sugar and cinnamon if desired.

makes 6 to 8 doughnuts

Chow-Chow

Nut Brownies

Maple Syrup Cake

Wellesley Fudge Cake

✄ Nut Brownies

4 squares unsweetened baking chocolate
1 cup butter, cut into pieces
2 cups sugar
4 eggs
1½ cups flour
¼ teaspoon salt
1½ teaspoons pure vanilla extract
1½ cups coarsely chopped walnuts or pecans

Preheat oven to 375°.

Melt the chocolate in the top of a double boiler over hot but not boiling water. Add the butter gradually, stirring well after each addition. Add the sugar and stir until completely melted. Remove from heat.

Add the eggs, 1 at a time, beating well after each addition. Beat in the flour, salt and vanilla extract. Add the nuts and stir.

Pour the batter into a buttered and floured 9 × 9 × 2-inch square baking pan. Bake for 40 minutes or until the brownies begin to shrink away from the sides of the pan. Cool in pan, then cut into squares.

makes 16 to 20 brownies

✄ Holiday Plum Pudding

½ cup flour, sifted
1 teaspoon ground cinnamon
½ teaspoon baking soda
½ teaspoon ground cloves
¼ teaspoon salt
¾ cup unflavored bread crumbs
8 tablespoons unsalted butter
¾ cup light brown sugar
3 eggs
1½ pounds pitted purple plums, canned or fresh
2 tablespoons grated orange rind
½ pound pitted dates, chopped
1 cup white raisins
1 cup chopped pecans
½ cup black currants

Mix the flour, cinnamon, baking soda, cloves, salt and bread crubs together in a bowl.

Cream the butter and brown sugar together, then beat in the eggs one at a time. Drain the plums and chop them into small pieces. Using a wooden spoon, stir the plums and orange rind into the butter-sugar mixture. Gradually blend in the flour mixture until smooth. Fold in the dates, raisins, pecans and currants. Lightly butter a 2-quart pudding mold. Spoon the mixture into the mold and cover tightly with the mold's lid or aluminum foil. Place a steaming rack or a small, oven-proof bowl turned upside-down in a large pot. Put the pudding mold on the rack or bowl, and add enough boiling water to the pot to reach halfway up the sides of the mold. Cover the pot tightly and steam over low heat for 4½ hours, or until the pudding is very firm.

Cool the pudding in the mold, then loosen it around the edges with a knife. Invert the mold onto a serving plate and let the pudding cool for at least 15 minutes. Serve each portion topped with Pudding Sauce (see below).

serves 15 to 18

✄ Pudding Sauce

3 ounces cream cheese
1 egg
1 cup confectioner's sugar
2 tablespoons butter
1 teaspoon lemon juice
⅛ teaspoon salt
1 cup whipping cream
3 tablespoons dark rum

Use a fork or electric beater to soften the cream cheese until it is light and smooth. Mix in the egg, sugar, butter, lemon juice and salt and blend together. Whip the cream until it is thick. Fold it into the mixture. Fold in the rum. Chill.

113

Desserts

✣ Cider Pudding with Hard Sauce

½ cup almonds
¾ cup unflavored bread crumbs
4 eggs, separated
¾ cup sugar
1 teaspoon grated lemon peel
½ teaspoon cinnamon
¼ teaspoon grated nutmeg
¼ teaspoon salt
1½ cups apple cider
Hard Sauce (see below)

Preheat the oven to 350°.

Grind the almonds and bread crumbs together in a blender or food processor.

In a mixing bowl, beat the egg yolks until light and fluffy. Add the sugar and beat until smooth and blended, about 3 minutes. Stir in the lemon peel, cinnamon, nutmeg, salt and almond–bread crumb mixture. Blend well.

In a separate bowl, beat the egg whites until they are stiff but not dry. Fold them into the egg yolk mixture.

Pour the batter into a buttered 1½-quart casserole. Bake 25 to 30 minutes, or until the pudding is brown and firm to the touch. Remove from oven.

Heat the cider thoroughly in a saucepan but do not boil. Pour the hot cider over the pudding while it is hot. Let stand for 10 minutes. Serve hot or cold with Hard Sauce (see below).

serves 8

✣ Hard Sauce

⅓ cup butter, softened
1 cup confectioner's sugar
2 tablespoons dark rum

In a mixing bowl combine the butter and confectioner's sugar. Mix until well blended and smooth. Add the rum and stir well.

✣ Indian Pudding

3 tablespoons yellow corn meal
⅓ cup dark molasses
3 cups milk, scalded
½ cup sugar
1 egg, beaten
1 tablespoon butter
¼ teaspoon salt
½ teaspoon ground ginger
½ teaspoon cinnamon
1 cup cold milk

Preheat the oven to 300°.

Scald the milk in a saucepan. Stir in the corn meal and molasses. Cook over low heat until mixture thickens, stirring constantly.

Remove the saucepan from the heat and add the sugar, egg, butter, salt, ginger and cinnamon.

Pour the mixture into a buttered baking dish or casserole and bake for 30 minutes. After 30 minutes, pour the cold milk into the baking dish. Do not stir. Continue baking for 2 more hours. Serve the pudding warm with lightly sweetened whipped cream.

serves 6 to 8

✣ Cranberry Snow

2 cups fresh cranberries
4 cups water
1½ cups sugar
1 teaspoon lemon juice

114

Wash the cranberries. Place them in a 3-quart saucepan with the water and bring to a boil over high heat. Reduce the heat, cover the saucepan, and simmer for 10 to 12 minutes or until the cranberries can be easily mashed.

Purée the cranberries and their cooking liquid in a food mill, blender, or food processor. Alternatively, press them through a sieve with the back of a spoon.

Place the cranberry purée in a glass or ceramic (not metal) bowl and add the sugar and lemon juice. Stir well.

Remove the dividers from 2 ice-cube trays. Pour the mixture into the trays. Freeze the cranberry mixture for 3 to 4 hours, stirring with a fork every 5 minutes or so to break up the solid particles that form. Serve in individual dessert cups.

serves 8 (makes 1 quart)

✂ Rhubarb Pie

2 cups cut-up rhubarb
1½ teaspoon salt
½ teaspoon salt
1½ tablespoons cornstarch
1 egg, beaten
2 tablespoons butter
pastry for 2-crust, 9-inch pie

Preheat the oven to 425°.

Cut the rhubarb into 1-inch pieces. Do not peel. Place the pieces in a bowl and cover them with boiling water for 1 minute. Drain well and reserve.

Combine the sugar, salt and cornstarch together in a mixing bowl. Add the egg and the rhubarb.

Place 1 of the pastries into a 9-inch pie plate. Fit well and crimp. Fill the shell with the rhubarb mixture and dot with butter.

Cut strips of dough with a sharp knife or pastry wheel from the second pastry. Make a lattice across the top of the pie plate and crimp the edges.

Bake for 35 to 40 minutes or until the rhubarb is tender. Cool before serving.

serves 8

✂ Apple Rum Pie

1 pastry for 2-crust, 9-inch pie
1 cup light brown sugar
¾ teaspoon cinnamon
¼ cup flour
⅛ teaspoon salt
6 cups peeled, cored and thinly sliced apples
2 tablespoons butter, cut into small pieces
2 tablespoons dark rum

Preheat the oven to 425°.

Roll out the pastry on a lightly floured surface. Fit half of it into a 9-inch pie plate.

In a small bowl combine the sugar, cinnamon, flour and salt.

Place the sliced apples in a large bowl. Add the sugar mixture and mix lightly. Place the apple-sugar mixture into the pie shell and dot with butter.

Roll out the remaining pastry on a lightly floured surface. Make slits in the center and fit it over the filling. Seal the edges together, trim, and flute.

Bake for 45 to 50 minutes or until the crust is golden. Remove from the oven to a cooling rack. Pour the rum through the center slits. Cool on rack until warm and serve.

serves 6 to 8

Apple Dumplings

2½ cups flour
3 teaspoons baking powder
1 teaspoon salt
3 tablespoons sugar
⅔ cup butter
½ cup milk
2 tablespoons butter
⅔ cup light brown sugar
¾ teaspoon cinnamon
¼ teaspoon freshly grated lemon peel
6 medium-sized apples, peeled and cored

Preheat the oven to 350°.

In a large bowl combine the flour with the baking powder, salt and sugar. Cut in the ⅔ cup butter with a pastry blender or two knives until the mixture resembles a coarse meal. Add the milk gradually. Mix gently and shape the dough into a ball.

In a small bowl combine the 2 tablespoons butter, brown sugar, cinnamon and lemon peel.

Turn the dough out on a lightly floured surface and roll it out into a 13 × 20-inch rectangle. With a pastry wheel or sharp knife, cut the dough into six squares.

Place an apple in the center of each square. Spoon the brown sugar mixture evenly into the cored centers. Moisten the edges of the pastry and bring the four corners up and over the apples. Press the corners together to secure. Cut small gashes into the sides of the pastry.

Place the encased apples into a buttered baking dish. Bake for 40 to 45 minutes or until the pastry is golden. Serve warm with whipped cream.

serves 6

Concord Grape Pie

5 cups Concord grapes
water
1 cup sugar
1 tablespoon lemon juice
¼ cup flour
⅛ teaspoon salt
1 pastry for 2-crust, 9-inch pie
heavy cream

Preheat the oven to 400°.

Roll half the pastry out onto a lightly floured suface. Fit it into a 9-inch pie pan and set aside.

Remove the skins from the grapes. This is best done by pinching the end opposite the stem and squeezing the grape out. Reserve the skins.

Place the skinned grapes in a saucepan with enough water almost to cover them. Quickly bring to a boil. Reduce the heat and simmer for 3 to 4 minutes or until the grapes are soft. Push the grapes through a sieve with the back of a spoon and discard the pits.

In a bowl combine the grape pulp, grape skins, sugar (use more if the grapes are very tart), lemon juice, flour and salt. Mix well and pour into the pie crust.

Top the pie with the second crust. Seal and flute the edges. Cut steam vents in the top. Brush the top with heavy cream and sprinkle with sugar.

Bake for 40 minutes. Cool before serving.

makes 1 9-inch pie

Rice Pudding

3 cups milk
1 cup light cream
4 teaspoons uncooked rice
2 tablespoons water
¼ teaspoon salt

Preheat the oven to 250°.

Pour the milk and cream into a lightly buttered medium-sized baking dish or casserole. Stir in the rice, sugar and salt.

Place the baking dish in the oven for 3 to 4 hours. Stir frequently, but not during the last 30 minutes of baking time. Test the rice for tenderness at the end of 3 hours. The pudding will be thin when it is taken from the oven.

Allow the pudding to cool before serving. It will thicken as it cools.

serves 4

❄ Buttermilk Raisin Cake

½ cup butter
1 cup sugar
3 eggs, separated
½ cup buttermilk
2 tablespoons prune juice
2 cups flour
½ teaspoon baking soda
1 heaping cup raisins, chopped

Preheat the oven to 350°.

In a mixing bowl cream the butter and sugar together until light and fluffy.

In a separate bowl beat the egg yolks. Stir them into the butter and sugar mixture. Add the flour and baking soda and stir well.

In a small bowl beat the egg whites until they are stiff but not dry. Fold gently into the batter. Stir in the raisins.

Turn the batter into a buttered 9-inch square baking pan. Bake for 35 to 40 minutes or until a cake tester inserted into the center comes out clean. Cool on a rack before serving.

makes 1 cake

❄ Pound Cake

1 pound butter
1 pound sugar
10 eggs, separated
4 cups flour
½ teaspoon salt
1 teaspoon baking powder
1 teaspoon pure vanilla extract
2 tablespoons freshly grated lemon rind

Butter two 12-inch loaf pans and dust them lightly with flour. Set aside.

In a large bowl cream the butter. Gradually add the sugar and continue creaming until the mixture is light and fluffy.

In a separate bowl beat the egg yolks. Add the yolks to the butter mixture, beating constantly.

In a bowl or on a large sheet of waxed paper, sift together the flour, salt, and baking powder four times.

Gradually add the flour to the butter mixture. Mix thoroughly. Add the vanilla and lemon rind. Mix thoroughly.

Preheat the oven to 300°.

In a small bowl beat the egg whites until they are stiff but not dry. Fold into the batter.

Pour half the mixture into each of the loaf pans. Bake for 1 to 1¼ hours or until a cake tester inserted into the middle of the loaf comes out clean.

Remove to cooling racks. Cool 10 minutes in the pan. Then turn out onto racks and cool completely.

A traditional pound cake such as this one calls for one pound each of the major ingredients. Ten eggs weigh about one pound.

makes 2 loaf cakes

117

❧ Condiments ❧

Thrifty New England housewives in the days before refrigeration were famous for their pickles, relishes, preserves and other condiments. These concoctions preserved the bounty of the summer harvest for the winter. And although the cooks of the time didn't know it, they were also preserving important vitamins for a time when fresh fruits and vegetables would be scarce. The captains of fishing and whaling ships, for example, knew that cranberries preserved in jellies and relishes helped prevent scurvy among the crew, even if they didn't know that cranberries are rich in Vitamin C.

A number of recipes for traditional New England condiments such as Chow-Chow are given here. Serve these along with roasted meat or poultry (hot or cold), as an accompaniment to a sandwich lunch, or just with some home-baked bread as a snack. When packed in an attractive jar, homemade condiments are also an excellent gift from your kitchen.

❧ Tartar Sauce

1 cup mayonnaise
2 tablespoons chopped pickle
1 tablespoon chopped green olives
2 teaspoons chopped onions
1 tablespoon chopped parsley
1 teaspoon mustard (optional)

In a bowl combine the mayonnaise, pickle, olive, onions, parsley and mustard. Combine thoroughly. Use immediately or refrigerate until needed.

makes 1 cup

❧ Golden Jam

2 large thin-skinned oranges
6 cups diced rhubarb
3 cups finely chopped carrots
4 cups sugar

Halve the oranges and remove the seeds. Finely chop the oranges with the peel.

In a large pot combine the oranges, rhubarb, carrots and sugar. Let the mixture stand overnight.

Bring the mixture to a boil. Reduce the heat and cook slowly until the rhubarb is transparent and the mixture is thickened.

Pour into hot sterilized glass jars. Seal and cool.

yields 10 8-ounce jars

❧ Spicy Plum Jam

6 pounds ripe plums
9 cups sugar
½ teaspoon cinnamon
¼ teaspoon ground cloves
¼ teaspoon ground ginger
¼ cup vinegar

Halve and pit the plums, but do not peel them. Place the plums in a large pot. Add the sugar, cinnamon, cloves, ginger and vinegar. Bring slowly to the boil, stirring constantly. Simmer 40 to 45 minutes, stirring often.

When thickened, pour into hot sterilized glass jars. Seal and cool.

makes 2 quarts

❧ Chow-Chow

8 quarts green tomatoes, stemmed and chopped
8 large onions, chopped
10 green peppers, seeded and chopped
3 small hot red peppers, seeded chopped
3 tablespoons salt
1 quart vinegar
1 tablespoon cinnamon
¼ teaspoon ground cloves
3 tablespoons dry mustard
2 bay leaves
2 cups sugar
½ cup prepared horseradish

In a large mixing bowl combine the tomatoes, onions and peppers. Cover with the salt and let stand overnight. Drain the mixture well and put it into a large pot.

Add the vinegar to the pot. Tie the cinnamon, cloves, mustard, and bay leaves into a piece of cheesecloth and add to the pot. Add the sugar and horseradish. Bring the mixture to a boil and reduce heat. Simmer until the ingredients are tender, stirring frequently, about 15 minutes.

Place the mixture into sterilized glass jars. Seal and cool.

In the days of the China trade, the New England men who sailed on the fast clipper ships discovered Oriental foods, including a fruit preserve they called chow-chow. Eventually, the word came to mean this particular relish.

makes 7 to 8 quarts

❧ Pepper Cabbage Relish

1 cup chopped celery
2 cups chopped green peppers
1 medium-sized cabbage, cored and chopped
2 tablespoons cider vinegar
salt to taste
freshly ground black pepper to taste

Place the celery, green pepper, cabbage, vinegar, salt and pepper into a large saucepan. Cook over medium heat, stirring occasionally, until the vegetables are tender.

Pour the mixture into sterilized glass jars, seal, and cool.

makes 3 pints

❧ Red and Green Pepper Hash

12 green peppers, seeded and coarsely chopped
12 sweet red peppers, seeded and coarsely chopped
12 large onions, coarsely chopped
3 tablespoons salt
boiling water
2 cups sugar
4 cups vinegar

Put the peppers and the onions into a large saucepan. Add the salt and cover with the boiling water. Let stand for 15 minutes. Drain well.

Add the sugar and vinegar to the peppers and onions. Bring the mixture to a boil and cook for 15 minutes.

Pour the mixture into sterilized glass jars, cool, and seal.

makes approximately 3 quarts

❧ Corn and Pepper Salad

24 ears fresh corn
1 medium-sized head cabbage, cored and finely chopped
2 onions, finely chopped
3 green peppers, finely chopped
3 sweet red peppers, finely chopped
2 cups sugar
2 tablespoons salt
3 tablespoons mustard seeds
5 cups distilled white vinegar

119

Cut the corn from the cobs with a knife.

Place the corn and chopped vegetables into a large saucepan. Add the sugar, salt, mustard seeds and vinegar. Bring to a boil. Reduce the heat and simmer for 20 minutes.

Remove from the heat and spoon into hot sterilized jars. Seal, cool, and store.

makes approximately 3 quarts

❧ Candied Cranberries

4 cups fresh cranberries
2 cups sugar
¼ teaspoon salt
¼ teaspoon baking soda
1 cup water

Place the cranberries, sugar, salt, baking soda and water into a large heavy saucepan. Bring the ingredients to a boil over medium heat. Cover and simmer gently for 15 minutes. Do not lift the cover during this time.

Cool, still leaving the cover on. Pour the mixture into sterilized glass jars and seal tightly. Store in the refrigerator.

makes approximately 4 cups

❧ Spiced Cranberry Jelly

4 cups cranberries
2 cups boiling water
1 cinnamon stick
3 whole cloves
⅛ teaspoon salt
2 cups sugar

Put the cranberries in a saucepan and add the boiling water, cinnamon stick, cloves and salt. Bring the water to a boil again over medium heat. Cover the saucepan and cook the cranberries until the skins burst, about 3 to 4 minutes.

Drain the cranberries. Push them through a sieve into a saucepan, discarding any solids that remain in the sieve.

Stir the sugar into the cranberry juice. Bring the liquid to a rapid boil and cook for 2 minutes. Remove the saucepan from the heat and cool. Remove the cinnamon stick and cloves before serving.

makes about 2 pints

❧ Orange and Cranberry Relish

3 small thin-skinned oranges, unpeeled
1 cup fresh cranberries
sugar to taste

Shred the oranges and cranberries by placing them in a blender or food processor for 10 to 15 seconds or by putting them through the coarse blade of a grinder.

Place the oranges and cranberries in a bowl. Add sugar to taste, but keep the mixture on the tart side.

Place in a covered jar and chill for 24 hours.

makes approximately 1 pint

❧ Molded Cranberry Sauce

2 cups water
2 cups sugar
4 cups cranberries
2 teaspoons grated orange rind

Put the water and sugar into a saucepan. Stir until the sugar is dissolved. Bring the mixture to a boil over medium heat and cook for 5 minutes.

Add the cranberries to the syrup and simmer very gently until the sauce is thick, about 5 minutes. Do not stir while the sauce cooks. Skim the surface of the sauce and stir in the orange rind.

Pour the sauce into 1 large or 3 or more small molds. Chill until the sauce is firm. Carefully unmold and serve.

makes 1 large or 3 small molds

✻ Apple Butter

8 cups apple cider
3½ pounds cooking apples, cut into eighths
3 cups sugar
½ teaspoon ground cloves
1 tablespoon cinnamon
¼ teaspoon salt

Place the apple cider in a large saucepan. Bring to a boil and boil for 15 minutes. Add the apples to the pot and cook until very tender.

When done, force the apples through a sieve with the back of a spoon. Put the sieved apples back into the saucepan; discard the peels and seeds in the sieve. Add the sugar, cloves, cinnamon and salt. Simmer slowly until thick, stirring frequently to prevent burning. Pour into jars or crock.

makes 4 pints

✻ Citrus Conserve

6 oranges
5 cups water
6 cups sugar
¼ cup lime juice
1 2-inch cinnamon stick
½ cup seedless raisins

Wash and quarter the oranges. Remove the peel. Chop the pulp finely, discarding the membranes and seeds.

Chop the peel finely in a food chopper, blender or food processor. Place the peel in a saucepan, cover with the water and bring to a boil. Lower the heat to medium and cook until the peel is tender, about 20 minutes. Add the orange pulp and juice and cook 20 minutes longer, or until the mixture has cooked down to half its original volume.

Add the sugar, lime juice, cinnamon and raisins. Cook, stirring constantly, until the sugar is totally dissolved, about 30 minutes.

Remove from the heat. Carefully spoon the mixture into hot sterilized jars. Seal, cool, and store.

makes approximately 3½ pints

✻ Blueberry Relish

1½ quarts fresh blueberries
1 apple, peeled, cored and finely chopped
½ cup sugar
1 cinnamon stick
1 teaspoon whole cloves
4 teaspoons lemon juice
2 teaspoons Angostura bitters

Place the blueberries into a large saucepan. Stir in the apple, sugar, cinnamon and cloves. Bring the mixture to a boil. Reduce the heat and simmer for 3 to 4 minutes. Add the lemon juice, vinegar and bitters. Stir until just mixed. Remove from the heat and cool.

When the mixture has cooled completely, pour it into a strainer. Reserve the syrup. Discard the cinnamon stick and cloves. Chill the solid relish left in the strainer. It will keep well for 7 to 10 days in the refrigerator. Use the syrup to glaze a small ham.

makes 1½ cups

❅ Old-Fashioned Strawberry Jam

6 cups hulled strawberries
3 cups sugar

Place the strawberries into a large, heavy pot and mash them. Cook over moderate heat until the pulp is fairly thick, stirring often. Gradually add the sugar. Continue cooking over low heat until the sugar is dissolved. Stir constantly. Bring the mixture to a boil and boil rapidly for 15 to 20 minutes.

Skim the mixture and pour it into hot sterilized glass jars. Seal and cool.

makes 4 8-ounce jars

❅ Raspberry Currant Jam

3 cups currants
2 cups crushed raspberries
3 cups sugar

Place the currants in a saucepan and cover them with water. Cook until the currants are soft, about 5 to 7 minutes. Drain well. Press the currants through a fine sieve. There should be 2 cups of pulp.

In a saucepan combine the currant pulp, raspberries and sugar. Slowly bring the mixture to a boil. Stir occasionally until the sugar dissolves. Cook rapidly for 30 minutes or until the mixture reaches the jelling stage. Stir constantly as the mixture begins to thicken.

Carefully spoon the jam into hot sterilized jars. Seal, cool, and store.

makes 2 pints

❅ Strawberry-Rhubarb Jam

3 cups hulled strawberries
3 cups diced rhubarb
6 cups sugar

Place the strawberries in a large pot and mash them against the side of the pot with a wooden spoon. Cut the rhubarb into ½-inch pieces and add them to the pot. Mix well with strawberries. Add 4 cups of the sugar. Bring the mixture to a rapid boil and boil for 4 minutes.

Add the remaining 2 cups of sugar and boil again for 4 minutes. Pour into hot sterilized glass jars. Seal and cool.

makes 2½ pints

❅ Crabapple Jelly

5 pounds crabapples
sugar
1 teaspoon pure vanilla extract

Wash the crabapples. Remove the stem and blossom ends and cut the crabapples in half. Place the fruit in a large pot. Add enough water to cover and cook until the fruit is very soft, about 10 minutes.

Strain the mixture through a cheesecloth into another pot. Do not force the juice through the cloth. Measure the juice; there should be about 7 cups. For every cup of juice, stir in ¾ cup sugar. Discard the solids in the cheesecloth.

Bring the sweetened juice to a boil quickly. Cook rapidly until the juice begins to jell.

Skim off the foam, stir in the vanilla, and pour into hot sterilized glass jars. Seal and cool.

makes 4 8-ounce jars

❦ Cranberry-Pineapple Relish

1 cup water
4 cups fresh cranberries
1 cup dark raisins
2 cups sugar
½ teaspoon ground ginger
½ teaspoon cinnamon
¼ teaspoon salt
1 fresh pineapple, peeled and chopped

In a large saucepan, combine the water, cranberries, raisins, sugar, ginger, cinnamon and salt. Mix well and cook over medium heat until the cranberries start to pop and the mixture begins to thicken, about 20 minutes.

Stir in the pineapple. Continue cooking for an additional 20 minutes, or until the sauce has reached the desired thickness. Cool the relish and store it in a jar in the refrigerator. It will keep 1 to 2 weeks.

makes 1½ pints

❦ Tomato Ginger Preserves

1 pound ripe tomatoes
boiling water
1 pound sugar
2 lemons, thinly sliced and seeded
2 ounces candied ginger, chopped

Pour the boiling water over the tomatoes. Let stand briefly and drain well. With a sharp knife, remove the skins. Slice the tomatoes, cutting away the stem portion. Place the slices in a large bowl and cover them with the sugar. Let stand for 12 hours.

Drain the juice from the tomatoes into a saucepan. Bring the juice to a boil and cook until the syrup falls from a spoon in heavy drops, about 5 minutes. Add the tomato slices, lemon slices and ginger. Continue cooking until the preserves are thick and clear. Stir frequently.

Carefully spoon the preserves into hot sterilized jars. Seal, cool, and store.

makes 1 to 1½ pints

❦ Walnut Grape Conserve

4 pounds Concord grapes
5 cups sugar
grated rind of 2 oranges
juice of 2 oranges
⅛ teaspoon salt
1 cup seedless raisins
1 cup finely chopped walnuts

Wash the grapes and remove the stems. Peel the grapes by pinching the end opposite the stem and squeezing the grape out. Put the grape skins into a bowl and the peeled grapes into a saucepan. Cook the grapes over low heat for 5 to 8 minutes. Press the grapes through a sieve with the back of a spoon. Discard the seeds and solids left in the sieve.

Place the grape pulp back into the saucepan. Add the sugar, orange rind, orange juice, salt and raisins. Mix well. Cook over low heat, stirring constantly, until the sugar has dissolved. Raise the heat and bring the mixture to a boil. Stir constantly until the mixture is thick. Add the grape skins to the saucepan and cook 5 minutes longer or until the conserve is very thick. Remove from the heat and stir in the walnuts.

Carefully spoon the mixture into eight 6-ounce hot sterilized jars. Seal, cool, and store.

makes 8 6-ounce jars

✂ **Meal Planners**

Weekday Dinner

Yankee Vegetable Soup (page 21)
Escarole Salad (page 22)
Paprika Beef (page 76)
Potatoes with Mustard Sauce (page 34)
Succotash (page 36)
Apple Fritters (page 108)

Sunday Dinner

Cold Shrimp Cups (page 10)
Downeast Haddock Chowder (page 14)
Pork Chops with Apricot Stuffing (page 78)
Sweet Potatoes with Cranberries (page 45)
Broccoli Cheddar Casserole (page 28)
Parker House Rolls (page 97)
Blueberry Pie (page 105)

Christmas Dinner

Stuffed Clams (page 8)
Pumpkin Soup (page 21)
Green Salad with Honey Dressing (page 22)
Roast Goose with Fancy Fruit Stuffing (page 72)
Boston Baked Beans (page 24)
Acorn Squash with Rum Butter Glaze (page 35)
Orange and Cranberry Relish (page 120)
New England Honey Bread (page 94)
Holiday Plum Pudding (page 113)

New England Seafood Feast

Baked Oysters with Bacon (page 9)
Fruit of the Sea Chowder (page 14)
Boiled Lobsters (page 51)
Colonial Fish Pot (page 59)
Fried Asparagus (page 24)
Onions in Cream Sauce (page 30)
Anadama Bread (page 94)
Indian Pudding (page 114)

Summer Picnic

Lobster Salad (page 25)
Fruit and Chicken Salad (page 25)
Carrot Salad (page 25)
Maple Barbecue (page 82)
Smoked Pork Loaf (page 80)
Boston Brown Bread (page 93)
Chow-Chow (page 119)
Golden Jam (page 118)
Early American Apple Pie (page 106)
Hermits (page 103)

Weekend Brunch

Endive Salad (page 21)
Cheese Puffs (page 7)
Scrambled Oysters (page 55)
Fried Clam Cakes (page 48)
Old-Fashioned Raisin Bread (page 95)

Winter Game Dinner

Baked Bean Soup (page 12)
Baked Venison (page 80)
Sweet Potato Casserole (page 45)
Parsnip Fritters (page 32)
Cheddar Biscuits (page 97)
Pumpkin Pie I (page 105)

Buffet Supper

Deep-Fried Codfish Balls (page 7)
Scallop Brochettes (page 9)
Fried Clams (page 48)
Corn Pudding (page 28)
Puffed Shrimp (page 10)
Orange and Cranberry Relish (page 120)
Candied Cranberries (page 120)
Holiday Fruitcake (page 102)
Cranberry Snow (page 114)

Harvest Dinner

Pumpkin Soup (page 21)
Marinated Bean Salad (page 24)
Chicken with Crab-Meat Stuffing (page 69)
Pease Porridge (page 33)
Stuffed Acorn Squash (page 35)
Butter-Fried Dandelion Flowers (page 29)
Anadama Bread (page 94)
Apple Pandowdy (page 107)

Index